Web Programming with Go

Second Edition

Code, create, and troubleshoot every component of web application using Go and its libraries

Ian Taylor

GitforGits®
ASIAN PUBLISHING HOUSE

Published by: GitforGits

Publisher: Sonal Dhandre

www.gitforgits.com

Printed in India

First Printing: October 2025

ISBN: 978-93-49174-30-6

Cover Design by: Kitten Publishing

Prologue

The first edition was a huge success, which was really gratifying. It showed me how many developers are keen to create real Go web applications. I've had readers tell me about new projects they've started, how they've solved problems in production, and how they're enjoying learning something that actually works. When we were chatting and going through the editorials, one thing kept coming up: keep the practical examples, make the journey more friendly, explain real-world strategies, and don't forget what matters to someone coding at the keyboard.

That feedback shaped every page of this new edition. I tried to make each chapter as clear as possible, not just to polish the technical details, but to make sure each lesson fits into the bigger picture of building, securing, testing and growing full-featured web apps in Go. You'll see a clear theme throughout: clear code, honest advice, and the Bookstore project moving from an empty directory to a production-ready launch.

I'll be there with you as you set up workspaces, write your first handlers, connect databases, manage sessions and logins, and gradually tune your app for speed and reliability. I've included the lessons I wish I'd known my first month with Go, plus the methods and habits I still use today. Every step is designed to be actionable, so you can turn any concept into a feature.

This second edition isn't about complexity or rare scenarios, rather it's a focused journey for anyone ready to build, learn, and actually ship web applications in Go. I hope you find the process as rewarding as I have, and I'm looking forward to hearing how you've adapted these lessons and patterns to your own work.

Content

Preface

This is a new edition of "Web Programming with Go" and it's designed to help both entry-level and professional developers build and launch functional web applications using Go's core libraries. Every chapter gives you practical lessons, from setting up Go projects and building strong backend routes to frontend-backend integration, session management, authentication, concurrency, and connecting external APIs.

This book is a hands-on way to learn key skills like testing, logging, error handling and performance tuning, all explained in simple, direct language. The real code and examples make it easy to understand and use the concepts. It covers nearly every major aspect of Go web development, but keeps examples straightforward and avoids complex edge cases, making it ideal for learners and practitioners who want clarity and reliable progress. You'll learn to structure projects, design backend services, manage sessions, secure authentication, and integrate external APIs with step-by-step Bookstore examples. It's got clear, practical techniques for routing, concurrency, testing, logging, performance and error handling, and it uses code that's easy to understand and explanations that are easy to follow.

Basically, this book looks at modern Go features without getting into complicated or niche scenarios, making the lessons useful for real projects. This edition makes it easy for you to get from setup to deployment by focusing on simplicity over unnecessary detail.

In this book you will learn to:

- Get your web projects sorted with Go, using organised code, a modular design, and real-world workflows.
- You'll build, secure and test RESTful APIs using Go's net/http, Gorilla Mux and JSON best practices.
- Put in place user authentication, role-based access, and strong password protection to make sure your users have a safe experience.
- Get the front end and back end talking to each other by having clear API contracts and simple JSON data interchange practices.
- Use Go's concurrency tools to boost performance, scale up data fetching, and avoid deadlocks.
- Mock databases, APIs, and dependencies for fast, isolated, and reliable automated test routines.
- Set up session management, secure cookies, and resilient authentication flows to keep users logged in.
- Keep an eye on, log and trace application events to quickly find and fix problems.
- Use Go's HTTP client patterns to integrate payment gateways, external APIs, and third-party services.
- Come up with easy-to-understand error messages and stick to the standard incident response plans.

GitforGits

Prerequisites

This book is for every Go programmer and those who are eager to begin with Go and build web projects of their own interest, by leaveraging the various Go libraries and toolkits, that are made available by the Go community. All you need to begin with this book is some fundamentals around programming.

Codes Usage

Are you in need of some helpful code examples to assist you in your programming and documentation? Look no further! Our book offers a wealth of supplemental material, including code examples and exercises.

Not only is this book here to aid you in getting your job done, but you have our permission to use the example code in your programs and documentation. However, please note that if you are reproducing a significant portion of the code, we do require you to contact us for permission.

But don't worry, using several chunks of code from this book in your program or answering a question by citing our book and quoting example code does not require permission. But if you do choose to give credit, an attribution typically includes the title, author, publisher, and ISBN. For example, "Web Programming with Go, Second Edition by Ian Taylor".

If you are unsure whether your intended use of the code examples falls under fair use or the permissions outlined above, please do not hesitate to reach out to us at support@gitforgits.com.

We are happy to assist and clarify any concerns.

Acknowledgement

I owe a tremendous debt of gratitude to GitforGits, for their unflagging enthusiasm and wise counsel throughout the entire process of writing this book. Their knowledge and careful editing helped make sure the piece was useful for people of all reading levels and comprehension skills. In addition, I'd like to thank everyone involved in the publishing process for their efforts in making this book a reality. Their efforts, from copyediting to advertising, made the project what it is today.

Finally, I'd like to express my gratitude to everyone who has shown me unconditional love and encouragement throughout my life. Their support was crucial to the completion of this book. I appreciate your help with this endeavour and your continued interest in my career.

Chapter 1: Introduction to Web Development in Go

Introduction to Web Development

Something pretty significant happened at Google in 2007. Three seasoned (and pretty savvy) engineers, Robert Griesemer, Rob Pike, and Ken Thompson, came up with a plan to make web and systems development easier and more modern. With all the complexities of C++ and the verbosity of Java, it's no wonder that scaling things up quickly, and especially meeting the demands of modern web concurrency, can feel like a real challenge. And then, bam! Go showed up, and everyone's like, "Hey, we call it Golang."

The release of Go 1.0 in 2012 was a big deal for web engineering. A new language had come about, designed from the ground up to be clear, concise, and astonishingly effective for building web backends. We're moving on from the days of wrestling with complicated build tools and dependency nightmares. It's all about compositional design, strong concurrency, and easy-to-understand syntax. It made things easier for developers, not more complicated. People have been drawn to it ever since. Today, major tech companies use it to build and grow services that have to survive at internet-scale. As we go through this book, we'll keep coming back to this main mission: breaking down how to build real-world web apps with Go in a way that's easy to understand. We'll take it one step at a time, learning from the past as we create solutions for today.

Opportunities for Go

A web application today does not remain a simple website. Expectations have grown. That application must juggle thousands of concurrent users, interact seamlessly with cloud native tooling, and stay secure and performant all the while. Many languages attempt to meet these demands, but few achieve Go's elegance and practicality.

A significant reason for Go's ascendancy lies in its **compiled nature**. A Go binary runs directly on the machine, not inside a VM or with layers of indirection. Performance becomes immediate, and resource usage remains lean. An application built with Go launches nearly instantaneously and climbs briskly to serve the first request. The design of Go also provides us with **goroutines** which are the lightweight threads managed by the runtime, not the operating system. A single modern Linux server can readily support tens of thousands of these goroutines, allowing for concurrent handling of requests, background jobs, or data processing with minimal overhead. The channels permit safe, straightforward communication between these routines, banishing much of the pain associated with multithreading in other languages.

Another attention-worthy advantage is Go's **robust standard library**. Many essential components, from HTTP servers to cryptography to JSON handling, exist directly within the language's foundation. A major difference from some contemporaries is the lesser reliance on external libraries for routine tasks, translating to more reliable and secure deployments. Our web applications achieve more while remaining simple. There are several iconic organizations that have leaned on these strengths to build their platforms. The Docker's container technology depends on Go. Also the Kubernetes, the de facto standard for cloud orchestration, emerged from the flexibility and concurrency strengths of the language. Streaming and chat at Twitch require the same ability to handle massive numbers of frequent, fast concurrent connections. Likewise, Uber, Dropbox, and a litany of startups have recognized that Go's simplicity pays compound dividends as services scale.

A further architectural advantage of Go is its "**single binary**" deployment model. Once built, a Go application encapsulates everything into one executable. Most Linux server environments appreciate this, since deployments mean just copying a file and running it, instead of orchestrating interpreters, virtual environments, or elaborate setups. The containers in the Docker and Kubernetes world particularly benefit, like smaller images, less room for error, and faster startup. Apart from, many of us noticed early on that the code written in Go is easy to read, audit, and maintain. Short function signatures, minimal boilerplate, and predictable error handling allow teams to collaborate and evolve their projects with less friction. A team onboarding a new developer spends more time on product and less on deciphering the project structure.

Go's Features and Capabilities

This is a big step in our journey through web development with Go, and it comes with the release of Go 1.22. This latest version really ups the ante for Go's value proposition in building scalable, secure web services on Linux.

A few key features and enhancements in Go 1.22 (according to the official release notes: https://tip.golang.org/doc/go1.22):

- The introduction of improved error handling patterns produces code that remains clean while surfacing robust diagnostics. Errors can be wrapped, unwrapped, traced, and aggregated with renewed simplicity.
- Significant improvements in compilation and startup performance allow large web projects to build and launch with even greater speed.
- Changes to the net/http standard library endpoint add greater compliance with evolving web standards, including enhanced support for HTTP/2, finer request and response control, and easier connection management.
- Dependency management enjoys further polish. Go Modules now handle offline builds, proxy-less environments, and complex workspace arrangements with enhanced reliability.
- The toolchain advances. Diagnostic features, such as built-in race detection, improved code coverage analysis, and deeper profiling, empower web engineers to build safer and faster applications.
- Security defaults harden further, encouraging TLS by default and reducing chances for insecure configurations.
- Documentation and code examples, especially those targeting Linux server deployments, now reflect these best practices.

Within our practical references, every example, installation, and deployment guide targets Linux environments. Our code samples, shell scripts, and real-world exercises shall mirror the ecosystem found in today's Linux-powered web infrastructure.

Go Toolchain Essentials

The Go toolchain represents a suite of tightly integrated utilities created to simplify every aspect of the software development life cycle. The compiler sits at the heart of this toolchain, transforming the Go source code we write into blazing-fast machine code that runs natively on Linux. The experience of rapid builds and efficient, statically linked binaries has become synonymous with Go development.

The journey usually begins with the **`go build`** command, which compiles the project's main package, and, in a single, decisive step, resolves dependencies and produces a complete Linux executable. The **`go install`** command places built executables in standard locations, ready to run from anywhere. A newcomer to Go development may be surprised by how straightforward it is to create, update, and tidy up dependencies. The **`go get`** and **`go mod`** commands work hand in hand: new dependencies can be fetched with a single instruction, and **`go mod tidy`** cleans unused or obsolete references from our manifest, ensuring a minimal, reproducible set of requirements. A robust test framework, invoked via **`go test`**, sits alongside the compiler. In addition, the **`go bench`** command provides the means to run targeted benchmarks on any part of our codebase, supporting the performance-first mindset that has become second nature to Go programmers. The toolchain also includes helpers like **`go tool`** for fine-tuned performance tracing and analysis.

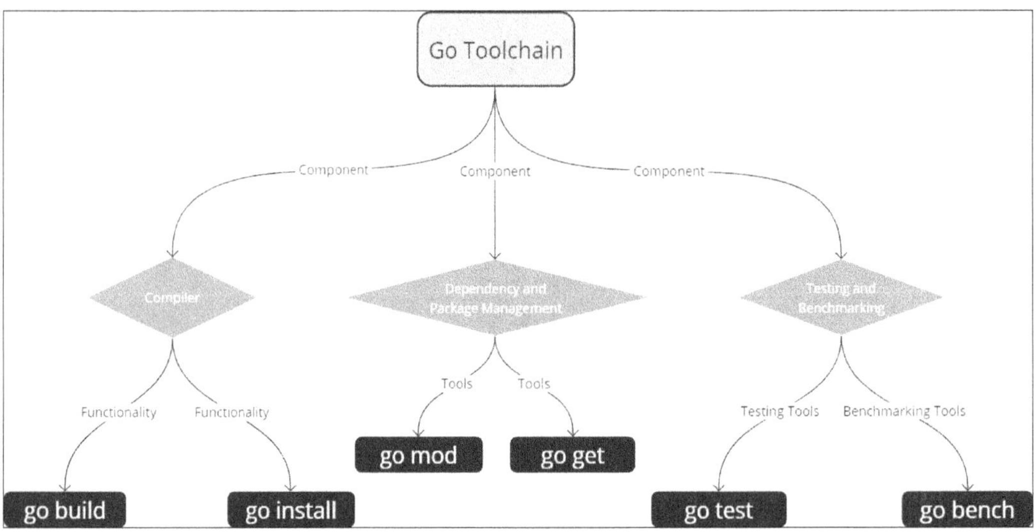

Fig 1.1 Go Toolkit

The essence of Go's toolchain is its philosophy of "batteries included, but not overwhelming." Every tool is available right from the standard distribution, on all major Linux distributions.

Setting up Go

A solid start always involves proper setup. Before developing any feature or web handler, our Linux environment needs Go installed. The Linux platform continues to be my preferred choice for both production servers and local development because of its performance, flexibility, and seamless compatibility with Go's build and deployment philosophies.

So, to install it on our Linux, we first navigate to the official Go downloads page and acquire the most recent Go archive suited for our usual architecture:

```
wget https://go.dev/dl/go1.22.0.linux-amd64.tar.gz
```

we then extract Go's archive to the **/usr/local** directory:

```
sudo tar -C /usr/local -xzf go1.22.0.linux-amd64.tar.gz
```

After this, we then add Go's binaries to your shell's search path by updating your profile configuration, along with a quick go install check:

```
echo "export PATH=$PATH:/usr/local/go/bin" >> ~/.profile
source ~/.profile
go version
```

This returns the installed Go version, and thereby confirms the system is ready for development.

Configuring Go Workspace

A well-organized workspace makes even the largest web projects manageable. Although Go Modules have done away with the rigid GOPATH workspace, the arrangement of the code directories with care remains a wise investment.

So here, we can create a typical structure for our bookstore project as below:

```
mkdir gitforgits-bookstore
cd gitforgits-bookstore
```

We then initialize the module:

```
go mod init github.com/gitforgits/gitforgits-bookstore
```

This above line creates the **go.mod** file, which is nothing but the module path and serves as the central ledger keeping track of dependencies and build settings. There are also organized subdirectories, like **cmd** for main application entry points, **pkg** for reusable packages, **internal** for private application logic, and **web** for static and template assets.

net/http

The net/http package sits at the core of Go's web development capabilities. As a part of the standard library, this package offers a plethora of functionalities, ranging from the basics of setting up a server and handling HTTP requests, to more intricate aspects like cookies, redirects, and file uploads. The true beauty of this net/http lies in its simplicity, abstracting away the complexities of the HTTP protocol while allowing developers to focus on the application logic.

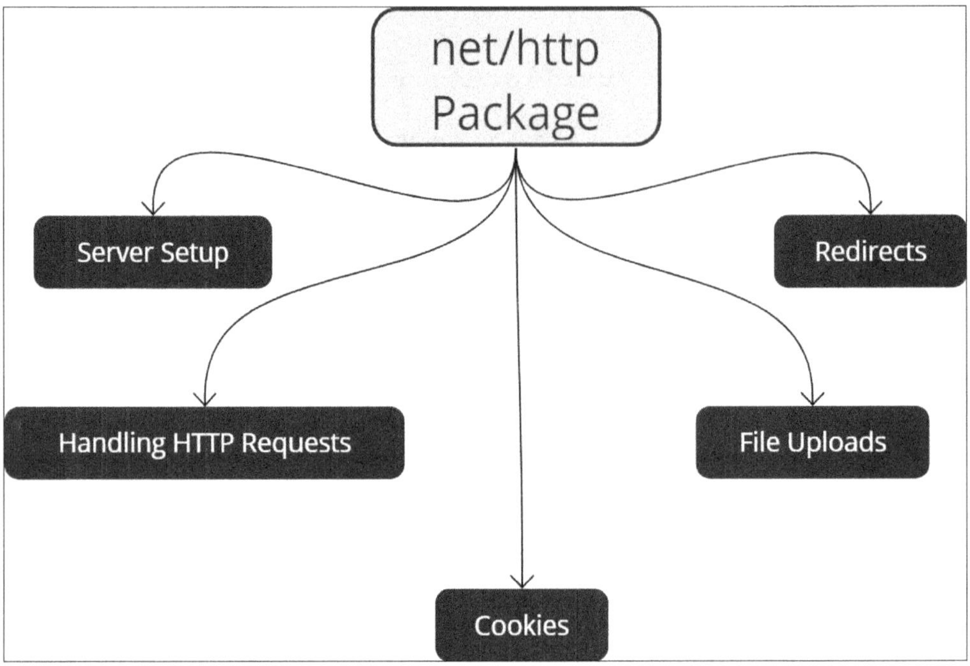

Fig 1.2 Overview of net/http Package

The dual capability of net/http to both function as an HTTP client and to set up HTTP servers is the core competency of this programming language. We can use it in our project, for which, we have to simply add the import statement: **`import "net/http"`**, and then we can leverage any functionality from this net/http package, like starting a server with **`http.ListenAndServe`** or crafting an HTTP client request using **`http.Get`**.

Setting up Web Server

Now that we're getting ready to bring the Bookstore application to life, picture us sitting at the same Linux terminal, with a mug of coffee next to the keyboard. We're all set to shape ideas into code. It's a blank directory, just waiting for some creativity and command-line magic.

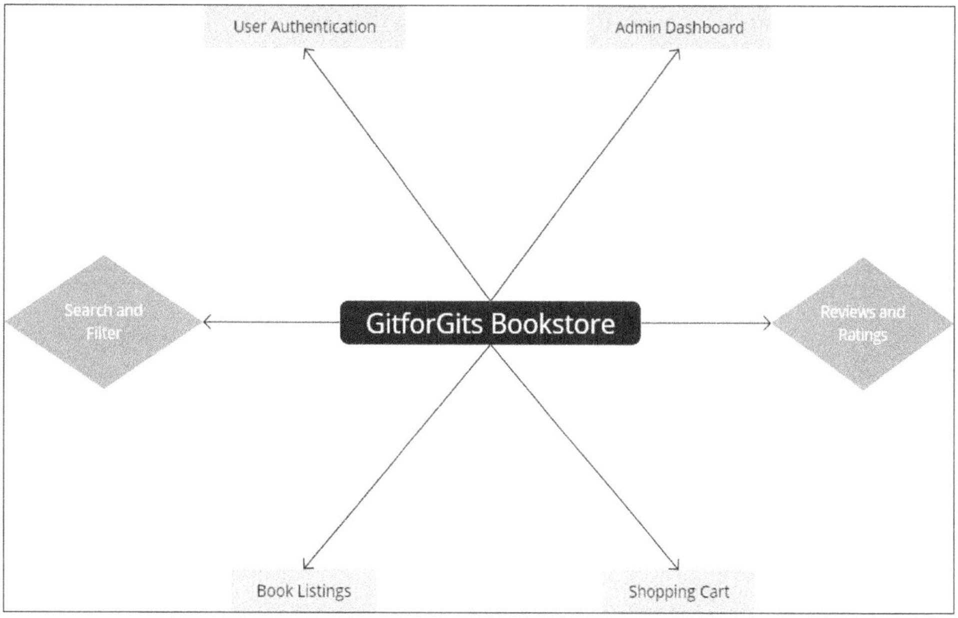

Fig 1.3 Functionalities of GitforGits Bookstore Application

The terminal prompt welcomes us. We'll decide on a folder for the project together. The name **"gitforgits-bookstore"** has a nice ring to it. It suggests a journey that connects our code to the world.

We can try entering:

```
mkdir gitforgits-bookstore
cd gitforgits-bookstore
```

After this, we then initialize our project as a module. This will help us easily manage dependencies and keep builds reproducible and clean.

```
go mod init github.com/gitforgits/gitforgits-bookstore
```

Now here, a subtle thrill arises as the **go.mod** file appears. This file will become our codebase's passport, a simple document that opens doors to a world of open-source packages and tools. In addition, the Go's compiler rewards us with fast, self-contained binaries we can whisk away to live servers, often with a single **scp**.

Next, before we write our first code, we might pause and ask:

"Would it not be delightful to already imagine visitors browsing our Bookstore, each webpage served in milliseconds by the program soon to take shape?"

A moment most memorable in every developer's journey: seeing that first message beamed from the familiar glow of a browser, generated not by static files, but by a living web server written by us! So now, we bring up our VS Code with the Go extension and then create a file called **main.go**.

After creating the file, we then type the following:

```
package main

import (

    "fmt"

    "net/http"

)

func main() {

    http.HandleFunc("/", func(w http.ResponseWriter, r
*http.Request) {

        fmt.Fprintf(w, "Hello, GitforGits Bookstore!")

    })

    fmt.Println("The server is running at
http://localhost:8080/")

    err := http.ListenAndServe(":8080", nil)

    if err != nil {

        panic(err)

    }

}
```

Now here in the above code, the **fmt.Println** line gives us a warm welcome message, making our command line feel like a companion, not just a tool.

And then we run the file:

```
go run main.go
```

The message greets us:

```
The server is running at http://localhost:8080/
```

We then type the above address, and we can clearly witness the message "Hello, GitforGits

Bookstore!" that beams back at us. Our all future Bookstore development, framework and all, will be standing upon this very strong foundation.

Adding Routes to Bookstore

A single welcoming page forms a beautiful start, but a bookstore flourishes by offering many aisles, each with its own charm. We now find ourselves ready to add new paths to our web server, providing visitors with a broader experience and hints of the features still to come.

So now, we return back to our text editor, and we introduce a new handler function:

```
func aboutHandler(w http.ResponseWriter, r *http.Request) {
    fmt.Fprintf(w, "This Bookstore is crafted by passionate Go developers for an audience that loves learning!")
}
```

After this, we then extend our main function to create a tangible sense of growth as our codebase evolves:

```
func main() {
    http.HandleFunc("/", func(w http.ResponseWriter, r *http.Request) {
        fmt.Fprintf(w, "Hello, GitforGits Bookstore!")
    })
    http.HandleFunc("/about", aboutHandler)
    fmt.Println("The server greets you at http://localhost:8080/")
    err := http.ListenAndServe(":8080", nil)
    if err != nil {
        panic(err)
    }
}
```

And then finally, we save the file and restart our server:

```
go run main.go
```

We open our browser again to **http://localhost:8080/about** and a brief message returns, which very well confirms the project is setup successfully.

So far, I have enjoyed how I have taught and so I want you to try to build a simple **/contact** handler together. Following is the simple script:

```
func contactHandler(w http.ResponseWriter, r *http.Request) {
    fmt.Fprintf(w, "Reach out to us at contact@gitforgits.com. We love hearing from fellow Go enthusiasts!")
}
```

With this, a line is added to our routing in **main()**:

```
http.HandleFunc("/contact", contactHandler)
```

After this, you then restart the server and browse to **/contact**. You will for sure feel the application alive after you try it. The next topic will take us into the world of APIs, data, and richer user experience.

Our First RESTful Endpoint

When a bookstore is doing well, you can feel it. It's the energy of new arrivals, interesting sections, and information you can touch. In our Bookstore app, all the data moves through well-designed routes, so we can give users and future developers the info they need. It's time to share book data using modern APIs, creating connections between server logic and browsers, mobile apps, and other web services.

So in our app, any user arriving at **/books** will be expecting more than a message, like a list of available titles, their descriptions, and authors, and all these in a format ready for dynamic display or programmatic access. The JSON has become the universal language for web APIs. The Go's standard library handles JSON elegantly, requiring neither ceremony nor excess code.

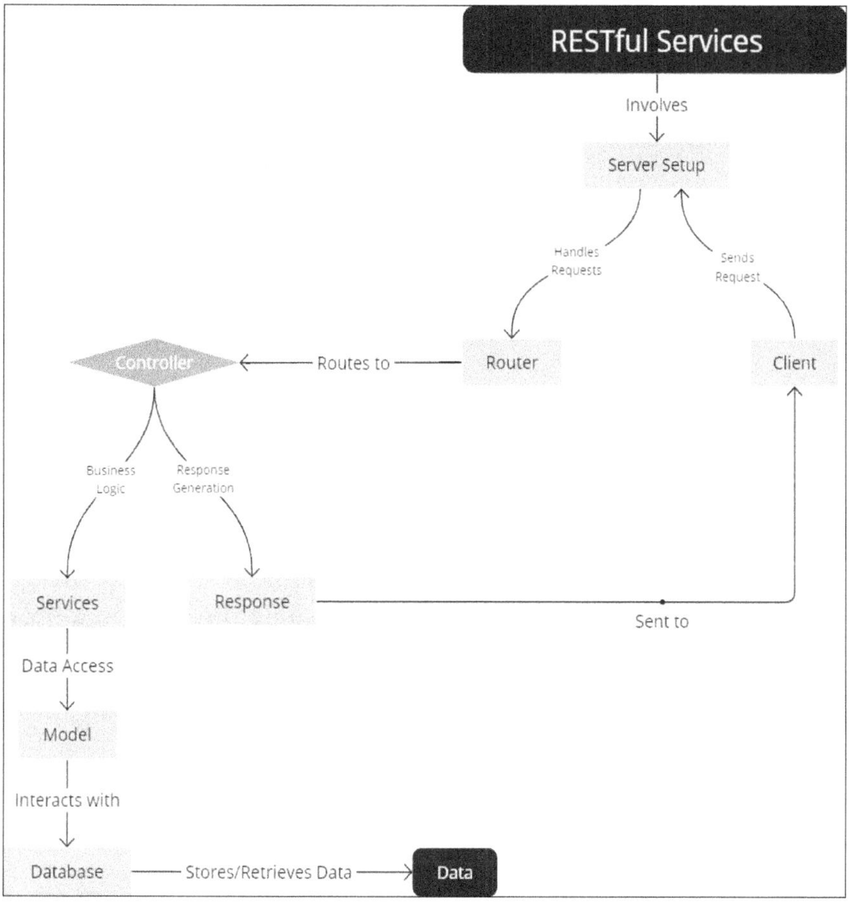

Fig 1.4 RESTful Services in Go

So here, the next task is to define a simple book type in our project. A Go struct stands ready to model each book's most relevant data. The code we write below waits in the **main.go** file after our handler functions.

```
type Book struct {
    ID     int    `json:"id"`
    Title  string `json:"title"`
    Author string `json:"author"`
}
```

An array showcases a sample inventory. The handler for our **/books** route displays this data, formatted for easy consumption by front-end developers or automated tools, as shown below:

```
func booksHandler(w http.ResponseWriter, r *http.Request) {
```

```
    inventory := []Book{
        {ID: 1, Title: "Go Basics", Author: "John Doe"},
        {ID: 2, Title: "Web Development with Go", Author:
"Jane Smith"},
    }
    w.Header().Set("Content-Type", "application/json")
    json.NewEncoder(w).Encode(inventory)
}
```

In our **main()** function, we then map the **/books** route accordingly:

```
http.HandleFunc("/books", booksHandler)
```

The server, once restarted, will show this new endpoint at **http://localhost:8080/books**. The user visiting this page in a browser can see a list of books in crisp JSON format. The joy of watching book information rendered live inspires us to think beyond our initial data. There will be new title releases, reviews, and user submissions, and all become possible when data flows freely, securely, and understandably.

Gorilla Mux for Advanced Routing

A web application flourishes when its routes reflect the needs and expectations of users. The initial paths in the Bookstore greeted visitors and presented some information using the simplest available approach. An expanding horizon now calls for a routing system that is as flexible as it is maintainable. This is the moment when Gorilla Mux, a respected routing library for Go, becomes an ideal collaborator in our journey.

The installation of Gorilla Mux in our system happens with just a single command:

```
go get github.com/gorilla/mux@latest
```

We can quickly have the update to our imports too:

```
import (
    "fmt"
    "net/http"
    "encoding/json"
    "github.com/gorilla/mux"
```

```
)
```

The main function transitions gracefully from basic routing to the powerful and expressive style provided by Gorilla Mux. The multiple routes can be easily configured with clarity as below:

```
func main() {
    router := mux.NewRouter()
    router.HandleFunc("/", func(w http.ResponseWriter, r
*http.Request) {
        fmt.Fprintf(w, "Hello, GitforGits Bookstore!")
    })
    router.HandleFunc("/about", aboutHandler)
    router.HandleFunc("/contact", contactHandler)
    router.HandleFunc("/books", booksHandler)
    fmt.Println("The server welcomes requests at
http://localhost:8080/")
    err := http.ListenAndServe(":8080", router)
    if err != nil {
        panic(err)
    }
}
```

Now here, the one valuable advantage of Gorilla Mux is its support for dynamic paths and parameters. Its design makes features like book lookups by ID not just possible but also elegant:

```
router.HandleFunc("/books/{id:[0-9]+}", singleBookHandler)
```

Inside the handler function for single books, Go retrieves parameters from the URL using Gorilla Mux's simple interface. This opens the door for detailed searches, custom data delivery, and personalized visitor interactions.

```
func singleBookHandler(w http.ResponseWriter, r *http.Request)
{
    vars := mux.Vars(r)
    id := vars["id"]
```

```
    // For demonstration, pretend to look up the book by ID
    book := Book{ID: 1, Title: "Go Basics", Author: "John
Doe"}
    if id == "1" {
        w.Header().Set("Content-Type", "application/json")
        json.NewEncoder(w).Encode(book)
    } else {
        http.Error(w, "Book not found", http.StatusNotFound)
    }
}
```

In the above, the code base now mirrors a growing store, where every shelf and aisle responds intelligently to the needs of its guests.

Establishing Environment Configuration

There are some things you need to be able to do with a reliable web application. For example, you need to be able to adjust settings and secrets without changing the source code. But as the Bookstore develops, it's starting to resemble other contemporary Go projects, with an emphasis on environment configuration. This step makes sure our server can easily adapt to changes in database credentials, port numbers, or secret keys, especially when running on different Linux environments.

So here, I recommend the popular Go package for this purpose is **godotenv**. The installation integrates seamlessly with our Go Modules approach:

```
go get github.com/joho/godotenv@latest
```

The creation of a **.env** file in our project directory offers space for variables in key-value form:

```
PORT=8080
DATABASE_URL=postgres://user:password@localhost:5432/bookstore
SECRET_KEY=myverysecretkey123
```

The Go's code utilizes **godotenv** to read these settings before launching the server:

```
import (
```

```
    "fmt"
    "os"
    "github.com/joho/godotenv"
)
func loadEnv() {
    err := godotenv.Load()
    if err != nil {
        fmt.Println("Could not load .env file, using default
settings.")
    }
}
```

The **main()** function now calls **loadEnv()** at the start. The port and other variables are read directly from the environment:

```
func main() {
    loadEnv()
    port := os.Getenv("PORT")
    if port == "" {
        port = "8080"
    }
    router := mux.NewRouter()
    router.HandleFunc("/", homeHandler)
    router.HandleFunc("/about", aboutHandler)
    router.HandleFunc("/contact", contactHandler)
    router.HandleFunc("/books", booksHandler)
    router.HandleFunc("/books/{id:[0-9]+}", singleBookHandler)
    fmt.Printf("The server welcomes requests at
http://localhost:%s/\n", port)
    err := http.ListenAndServe(":"+port, router)
    if err != nil {
```

```
        panic(err)
    }
}
```

This above environment-based configuration simplifies testing, deployment, and future feature expansion. These variables can be changed in a moment. There is no need to edit and recompile the code.

Summary

Overall, the Bookstore project, as developed so far, exhibits many strengths of Go as a language and platform for modern Linux-based web development. Our journey together in this chapter constructed the following milestones:

- The philosophy and historical roots of Go.
- Steps for setting up Go 1.22 on Linux, with collaborative attention to workspace and project structure.
- Simple yet powerful HTTP server handling, expanding with friendly routes.
- The adoption of Gorilla Mux for advanced routing and clean URL design.
- Implementation of environment configuration for real-world deployment scenarios.

To sum up, it was all about working together and having each other's backs. You could say that the process of building felt more like shared craftsmanship than rote instruction.

Chapter 2: Structuring Go Web Application

Explore Go Modules

The Bookstore application, as established in our previous chapter, I believe is able to craft a living example of how clear design and collaboration foster sustainable growth. The routes, handlers, and configuration patterns we built together prepare us for a new stage: organizing, maintaining, and sharing the project with confidence. The Go modules are a core innovation of recent Go versions. They transform the way web applications are structured and scaled on Linux. A module, at its essence, is a self-contained collection of Go packages, and each module signals to the Go toolchain such as, to our compilers, editors, and build servers.

Why Go Modules Matter?

When you're working on a professional web project, it's all about keeping things predictable and simple. These modules achieve this by:

- Making sure that every dependency is declared in a **`go.mod`** file inside the project directory.
- Controlling which library versions are used helps us avoid the chaos of unintended upgrades.
- Checksum verification (**`go.sum`**) for every external dependency helps boost security and trust.
- Supporting custom module proxies and version pinning, which helps with development in enterprise and cloud settings

It's all these benefits that make the Bookstore project reliable, give us confidence when we deploy updates, and make it easier for other developers to join in.

Setting up Bookstore Module

A new module begins with a simple process, always in a dedicated project directory. In this collaborative environment, we focus on transparency and repeatable steps:

```
mkdir gitforgits-bookstore

cd gitforgits-bookstore

go mod init github.com/gitforgits/bookstore
```

The result of running **`go mod init`** is a new **`go.mod`** file, typically appearing as:

```
module github.com/gitforgits/bookstore

go 1.22
```

This manifest records the module's name and the base Go version. As we add dependencies (for example, Gorilla Mux for routing, godotenv for configuration, or GORM for database management), the Go automatically updates this file to reflect the requirements.

Collaborating with Go Modules: Real Scenarios

Suppose we decide to include Gorilla Mux for robust routing. We import it into our code and run:

```
go get github.com/gorilla/mux@latest
```

The Go fetches the package, assigns a safe version, and adds it to both **go.mod** and **go.sum**. When another developer clones the Bookstore project and runs **go mod tidy**, their environment automatically receives the exact same dependencies.

Standard Go Directory Structure

A well-organized Go project is a lot like a well-designed bookstore. The structure sets the expectations for every reader or contributor who enters. When a project grows, not having a clear structure can lead to a lot of disorganized files, misunderstandings, and making onboarding new team members a hassle. On the other hand, well-structured code creates harmony, speeds up development, and lowers the risk of mistakes. A clear layout also helps us enforce security boundaries and embrace automation in how we deploy things, which is essential for production-grade applications running on Linux.

At the end of Chapter 1, our Bookstore web server consisted of a single **main.go** file (with handlers together, and a basic **go.mod**). For small tools or experiments, this works. However, as requirements expand, the support of new API endpoints, database integration, configuration, error handling becomes the urgent need for structure. So here, a scalable directory layout helps us prevent entropy as more scripts and features are added.

Standard Directory Layout

The Go does not force a single directory organization, but a set of conventions has emerged from successful real-world projects. These conventions guide our own Bookstore's structure, balancing clarity and scalability:

- cmd/ contains executable entry points. Each subfolder is a separate binary. Our main web server will live in cmd/bookstore/main.go.
- internal/ hosts application-specific packages and logic. Go restricts dependencies outside this repo from using internal, which enforces encapsulation. Here, we keep things like our HTTP handlers and business rules.
- **pkg/** is designed for code that could be reused in other projects. Utilities, common types,

and helpers fit here.

- **api/** defines our API schemas, OpenAPI specs, or, in advanced cases, Protocol Buffer descriptors.
- **web/** holds static assets (images, CSS, JavaScript) and HTML templates that our application might serve.
- **scripts/** stores Linux shell scripts for tasks like database migrations, build automation, or deployment.
- **database/** seed data for the database, or any DB-related assets.
- **docs/** gathers expanded documentation, architecture guides, onboarding files, or developer notes.

With such above folders, every responsibility in the application gets a clear home. If someone is fixing a server start bug, the search begins in **cmd/bookstore/**. To introduce a new API resource, then the work happens in **internal/handlers/** and gets documented in **api/**.

Establishing Project Structure

We will now begin applying the above structure. We get into the Linux terminal, inside our project root, and then create the folders in a single sweep:

```
mkdir -p cmd/bookstore internal/handlers internal/models pkg
api web scripts database docs
```

- **cmd/bookstore/** will host our **main.go**, the starting point of the web server.
- **internal/handlers/** will hold all our HTTP handler functions (think: logic for **/books**, **/about**, etc.)
- **internal/models/** will grow to store our data models (like a **Book** struct with methods attached).
- **pkg/** stands ready for any utility functions or types useful beyond this service.
- **api/** gives us a dedicated place for documenting the contract of our HTTP (or even gRPC) APIs.
- **web/** awaits our future HTML templates or front-end resources.
- **scripts/** and **database/** stand by for automation and migrations.
- **docs/** collects architectural and onboarding material.

A single main file becomes unwieldy if all routes, models, database logic, and configuration are mixed together. If we divide the code into purpose-specific directories, then:

- Each folder signals its intent. Any new team member knows where to locate business logic, handlers, or third-party code at a glance.
- The handlers in **internal/handlers/** can be unit-tested in isolation.
- The Go's **internal/** directory can prevent accidental or insecure imports from other modules or services.

As the Bookstore evolves, we keep on evaluate and adjust the layout accordingly. The large projects sometimes split the service into multiple repos: a core API, admin console, and background workers. Our conventions remain flexible by design, adjusting to the application's changing needs.

Package Management and Vendoring

We must rmember that the Bookstore project, like most real-world Go applications, relies on third-party libraries for routing, database interactions, configuration management, input validation, and more. A healthy project must make these external dependencies both manageable and predictable. If left unchecked, then the dependencies become a liability. The builds break as upstream packages change, the security risks appear when a new vulnerability emerges, and but obvious the team members waste time dealing with version mismatches or missing packages. Hence, a robust package management, along with a thoughtful strategy for vendoring, is much needed.

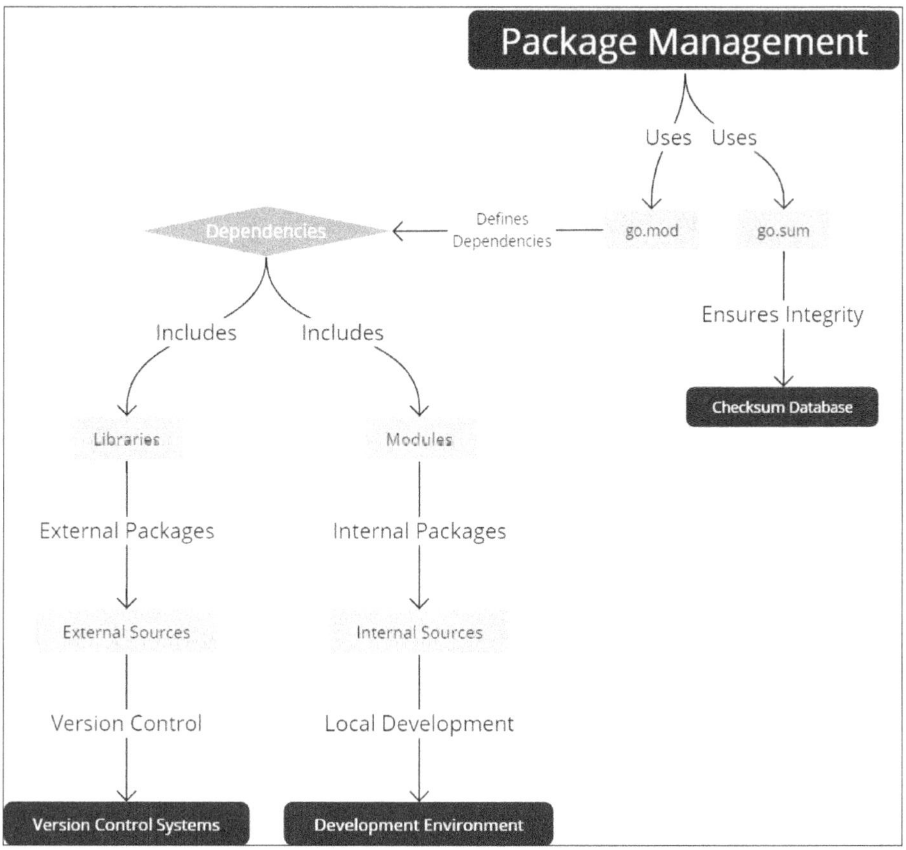

Fig 2.1 Package Management in Go

Adding and Updating Dependencies

Suppose the Bookstore needs improved routing, so we reach for Gorilla Mux. The process is both transparent and reliable:

```
go get github.com/gorilla/mux@latest
```

The Go fetches the requested version, updates the manifest, and saves the checksum. Does a new feature from a package become necessary, or a security fix arrive? The upgrade is simple:

```
go get github.com/gorilla/mux@v1.8.0
```

The change in **go.mod** makes every related file, test, and CI job aware. The presence of the accidental drift between development, testing, and production is eliminated.

Removing Dependencies

A project grows; and there are some features which are either replaced or dropped. Now, these unused packages clutter the module graph. So for this, the command:

```
go mod tidy
```

removes leftovers and prunes what is no longer needed, keeping the codebase lean. This habit protects both disk space and mental clarity.

What is Vendoring?

The function of vendoring is to copy all external dependencies (except the Go standard library) into a **vendor/** subdirectory within the project. At first glance, this might seem old-fashioned now that modules exist. However, the vendoring plays a crucial role in certain situations:

- If the build server or production environment lacks internet access, everything needed to build remains present inside the repo.
- Some organizations require reviewing the source of all dependencies. Having them locally in **vendor/** makes audits easier.
- If an author deletes or "yanks" a critical package, a vendored copy means the project can still be built.

In practicality, the creation of a vendor folder is both easy and safe:

```
go mod vendor
```

The build and the test with the vendored dependencies takes just one flag:

```
go build -mod=vendor
```

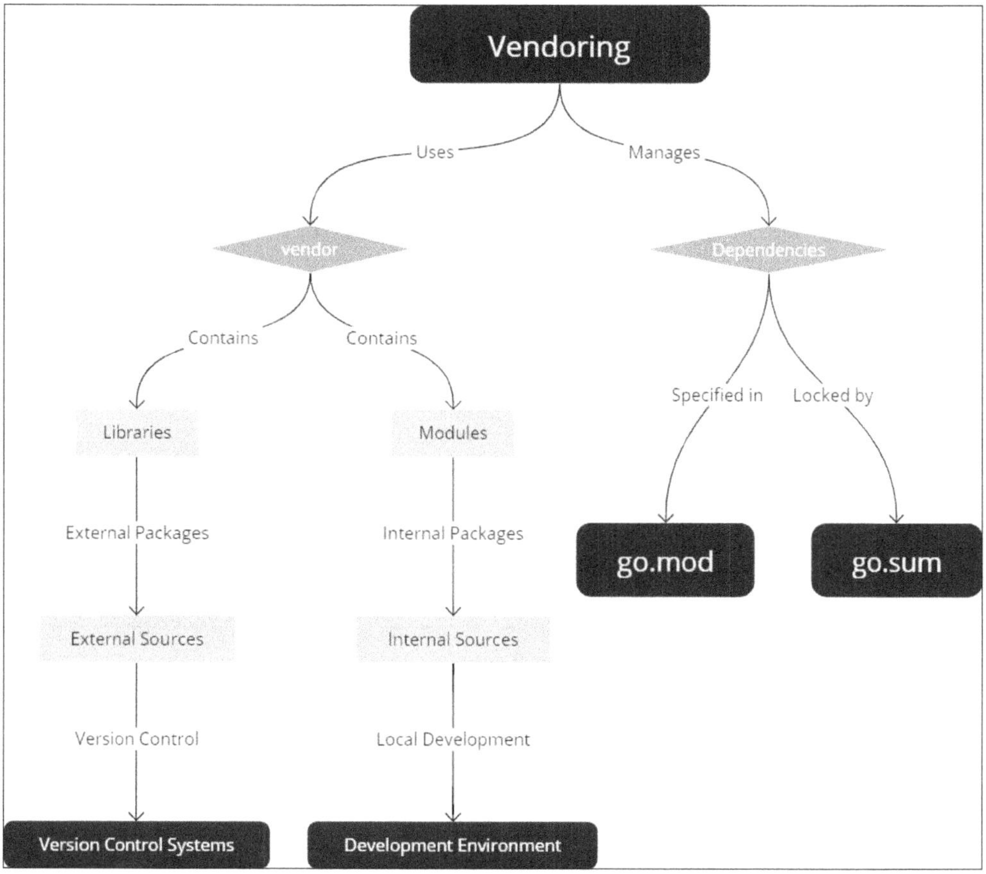

Fig 2.2 Vendoring in Go

The Go reads only from the local vendor folder rather than pulling from upstream sources. The team members, especially those in secure or regulated environments, expect every dependency to be available, readable, and version-locked. The vendoring provides exactly this. For open source projects, vendoring reduces "works on my machine" headaches, especially if contributors are in regions with unreliable connectivity.

Model-View-Controller (MVC)

Ww know one thing that without structure, the code becomes tangled, harder to maintain, and more prone to subtle bugs. The MVC pattern introduces a proven way to divide responsibilities, allowing teams to scale both features and contributors with confidence. The MVC architecture has since become a universal paradigm, especially for web applications.

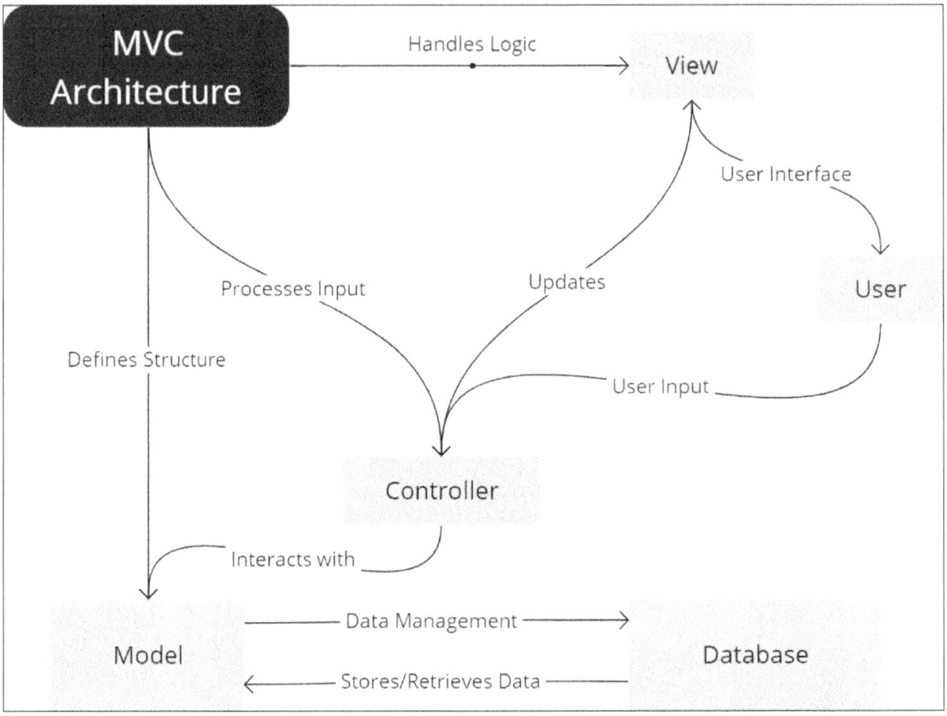

Fig 2.3 MVC Architecture in Go

The pattern divides core functionality into three cooperating components:

- **Model** which represents the data and business logic. Models define what a book is, store its properties, and provide functions for saving, updating, retrieving, or validating information.
- **View** manages how data is presented. Views generate HTML, JSON, or other output for web browsers and APIs. In API-driven Go projects, views are often rendered as JSON-encoding logic or templated HTML pages.
- **Controller** acts as the traffic cop, receiving HTTP requests, invoking the proper models, and deciding which view (output) to serve. Controllers manage application flow, orchestrating validation, business rules, and response formatting.

All three of these components have a specific role. They reduce code duplication and make it easy to change requirements without breaking unrelated sections.

MVC Suitability for Go

While some languages enforce MVC through heavyweight frameworks, the Go encourages a lighter, more explicit approach. Each major piece of logic lives in its own package or directory. For example, a typical Bookstore file layout might look like:

- **`internal/models/`** are the models like **`Book`**, **`Author`**, **`User`**

- **`internal/handlers/`** (the "controllers") are the functions mapped to URLs, handling HTTP requests for listings, user logins, or checkout
- **`web/templates/`** or **`internal/views/`** are the HTML templates or JSON response structures

The Go's explicit imports, modular file system, and static typing make MVC intuitive and error-resistant.

MVC Components in Bookstore App

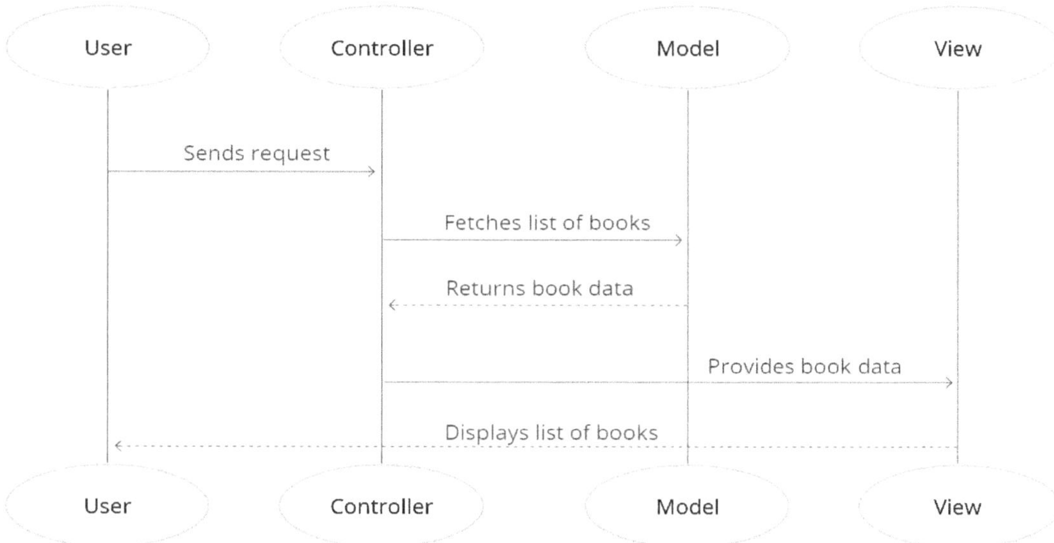

Fig 2.4 Application Flow

The Model

```
package models
type Book struct {
    ID      int
    Title   string
    Author  string
    Stock   int
    Price   float64
}
// Methods for CRUD (Create, Read, Update, Delete) operations
```

```
// and validation would be added here.
```

Here, a **Book** struct captures the essential data associated with an inventory item. Real-world projects add validation logic, database integration, and utility functions to the model layer.

The Controller (Handler)

```
package handlers
import (
    "net/http"
    "encoding/json"
    "bookstore/internal/models"
)
func ListBooks(w http.ResponseWriter, r *http.Request) {
    // In reality, we might fetch this from a DB
    books := []models.Book{
        {ID: 1, Title: "Go in Action", Author: "S. Ketkar",
Stock: 4, Price: 29.99},
    }
    w.Header().Set("Content-Type", "application/json")
    json.NewEncoder(w).Encode(books)
}
```

In the above, each handler connects to a model, processes any business logic, and writes the response using views (templates or encoders).

The View

For a web API, a view might be as simple as the JSON output in **ListBooks**. For HTML, Go's html/template package renders data as formatted web pages:

```
package views
import (
    "html/template"
    "net/http"
```

```
    "bookstore/internal/models"
)
var tmpl =
template.Must(template.ParseFiles("web/templates/book.html"))
func ShowBook(w http.ResponseWriter, book models.Book) {
    tmpl.Execute(w, book)
}
```

For each additional feature, like user registration, order history, admin dashboards, a similar division is replicated. The models own the business truth, controllers coordinate, and views display.

Programming Main Application Object

Why Application Object?

A larger web application, especially one aspiring to production use, cannot thrive solely on disparate handlers and loosely connected routes. The project needs a central "nervous system" which is nothing but an application object that orchestrates configuration, database connections, logging, and dependencies across controllers, models, and views. This object unifies the entire Bookstore, making operations like service startup, dependency injection, request flow, and graceful shutdown far more manageable.

The main application object, frequently called **App**, signals both the entry point and the brain of our architecture. Instead of passing configuration or connections around as global variables, we wrap them in the **App** struct and provide methods for initialization, lifecycle management, and routing.

Following are the features of Application Object:

- All shared resources, such as configuration, database connections, and loggers live in one place.
- Mocking or swapping out dependencies in tests is far easier.
- As features grow (e.g., caching, background tasks, metrics), they plug into the main object cleanly.
- Every part of the project knows where to look for vital services.

Designing Application Object

An initial design for the Bookstore's **App** struct may resemble:

```go
package main
import (
    "database/sql"
    "log"
    "net/http"
    "github.com/gorilla/mux"
    "os"
)
type App struct {
    Router      *mux.Router
    DB          *sql.DB
    Logger      *log.Logger
    Config      map[string]string
}
func (a *App) Initialize() {
    a.Logger = log.New(os.Stdout, "INFO: ",
log.Ldate|log.Ltime|log.Lshortfile)
    a.Config = map[string]string{
        "PORT": "8080",
        // Load others, possibly from env vars or .env
    }
    db, err := sql.Open("postgres", os.Getenv("DATABASE_URL"))
    if err != nil {
        a.Logger.Fatal("Could not connect to database")
    }
    a.DB = db
    a.Router = mux.NewRouter()
    // Register routes and handlers here
}
```

The struct gathers every essential resource. The initialization sets up logs, reads configuration, creates the database connection, and builds out all routes via Gorilla Mux.

As our Bookstore matures, the application object can manage more than initialization. Features such as graceful shutdown, metrics reporting, background task scheduling, and error recovery fit naturally within methods attached to **App**. The shift to an application object ensures every new feature and contributor can grow the project with confidence, without introducing hidden dependencies or unpredictable behavior.

Configuration and Environment Variables

A web application grows from a simple tool into a living system. At first, we might wire up a few routes, respond with messages or data, and see results nearly instantly. However, as features multiply, adding configuration, database connectivity, security checks, richer logging, or background tasks, the need for structured central control becomes obvious.

So here, the main application object is a possible solution. In Go, this typically means a struct, often named **App**, **Server**, or for us, perhaps **BookstoreApp** that stores all core services, configuration values, and long-lived resources. It becomes the cornerstone for dependency injection, modular routing, configuration management, and orderly startup and shutdown.

Implementing the App Object

We can start by outlining the struct:

```
package main
import (
    "database/sql"
    "log"
    "net/http"
    "os"
    "github.com/gorilla/mux"
    _ "github.com/lib/pq" // assuming Postgres; underscore for
side-effect import
)
type App struct {
    Router *mux.Router
    DB     *sql.DB
```

```
    Logger *log.Logger
    Config map[string]string
}
```

In the above,

- The router orchestrates incoming HTTP requests.
- The DB manages persistent storage (here, a SQL database; could be swapped with an interface for testing).
- The logger collects logs in a consistent way (we could later swap for structured logging).
- And, the config provides easy access to environment-driven settings so every handler and model stays in sync.

We now then proced to make the App object self-initializing:

```
func (a *App) Initialize() error {
    // Load config from environment variables or a .env file
    a.Config = map[string]string{
        "PORT": os.Getenv("PORT"),
        "DATABASE_URL": os.Getenv("DATABASE_URL"),
        // ...more config as needed
    }
    // Set up logging
    a.Logger = log.New(os.Stdout, "[Bookstore] ",
log.Ldate|log.Ltime|log.Lshortfile)
    // Initialize the DB connection
    db, err := sql.Open("postgres", a.Config["DATABASE_URL"])
    if err != nil {
        return err
    }
    a.DB = db
    // Set up the router with all routes
    a.Router = mux.NewRouter()
    a.setupRoutes()
```

```
    return nil
}
```

In the above, the configuration loading happens first, because almost every subsequent service depends on values like credentials or connection strings. The logging is ready as early as possible, ensuring issues even during startup are visible. And, the database connection is established and checked. Also the router is created and configured.

After this, there is a helper method, **setupRoutes()**, can centralize all route wiring in one place:

```
func (a *App) setupRoutes() {
    a.Router.HandleFunc("/books", a.ListBooks).Methods("GET")
    a.Router.HandleFunc("/books/{id:[0-9]+}",
a.ShowBook).Methods("GET")
    // ...more routes as needed
}
```

Next, the handlers can now also try to live as methods on the App object, not standalone functions. This makes every handler able to access shared resources directly.

Adding a Service

Suppose we want to send notification emails on order creation. So for this, we simply embed a mailer as below:

```
type App struct {
    ...
    Mailer MailerService
}
type MailerService interface {
    SendOrderConfirmation(to string, orderID int) error
}
```

The **Initialize** method would wire up the mailer, and order-related handlers can call **a.Mailer.SendOrderConfirmation** when appropriate. The tests would replace the MailerService with a mock.

Dependency Injection

When new features are added and the team grows, the codebase stays healthy only if different parts depend on clear contracts, not hardcoded implementations. That's where Dependency Injection (DI) comes in. Basically, DI is a way of writing code that's modular, testable, and flexible.

You can think of Dependency Injection as a way of providing resources or dependencies to an object, instead of making those dependencies yourself. It's not that the handler or controller is creating its own database connection or logger. Instead, those items are set up outside and passed in, usually at initialization. This makes the code easier to test, evolve, and reason about.

Types of Dependency Injection

The Go encourages explicitness, and this is where the DI commonly comes in two main forms:

1. **Struct-based injection**: Dependencies are set as fields of a struct (commonly our **`App`** object). They are initialized at the start and passed to all parts that need them.
2. **Interface-based injection**: Instead of storing a concrete type (like **`*sql.DB`**), an interface is used. This allows swapping databases (e.g., real Postgres vs. in-memory fake) for different use-cases or tests.

In the following we will explore both these above types in our Bookstore project.

Struct-based Injection

At first, we simply consider our **`App`** struct from earlier:

```
import (
    "database/sql"
    "log"
    "github.com/gorilla/mux"
)
type App struct {
    Router *mux.Router
    DB     *sql.DB
    Logger *log.Logger
}
```

We initialize the dependencies and set them:

```
app := &App{}
app.DB = dbConn    // where dbConn is created earlier with config
app.Logger = customLogger
app.Router = mux.NewRouter()
```

Any handler method that needs access to the logger or database simply can use the App's fields:

```
func (a *App) ListBooks(w http.ResponseWriter, r *http.Request) {
    // Use a.DB for queries
    // Use a.Logger to log the request
}
```

Now, since here there is no handler being tightly coupled to globals, the app can act as a hub for dependencies.

Interface-Based Injection

Suppose we want to test a handler without a real database, or support switching between a production DB and a stand-in. Go interfaces make this possible:

```
type BookStore interface {
    GetAllBooks() ([]Book, error)
    FindByID(id int) (Book, error)
}
```

We update App to use this interface:

```
type App struct {
    Router *mux.Router
    DB     BookStore     // Now an interface
    Logger *log.Logger
}
```

In production, we set **App.DB** to the real implementation:

```
app.DB = NewPostgresStore(os.Getenv("DATABASE_URL"))
```

For tests:

```
app.DB = NewInMemoryStore()  // a BookStore that works in-memory!
```

Handlers remain the same but are now highly testable.

Sample Program: Injecting a Mail Service

At first, let us consider that the Bookstore needs to email customers with order receipts. So here, we can start by defining a minimal interface:

```
type Mailer interface {
    SendMail(to, subject, body string) error
}
```

The app is extended:

```
type App struct {
    ...
    Mailer Mailer
}
```

Next, the initialization then wires up the correct mail service, like the real for production, and the mock for tests:

```
app.Mailer = NewSMTPMailer(os.Getenv("SMTP_CREDENTIALS"))
// or
testApp.Mailer = &FakeMailer{}
```

Now here, the handlers can just use **`a.Mailer.SendMail(...)`**, and noe more required to care about the underlying implementation.

Because dependencies are injected, the controller do not need to know the details of models, DB connections, or external services. The tests and future enhancements can focus on a single slice of logic. As we add code to **`internal/handlers/`** or integrate new modules, the App struct and injected interfaces become the glue that holds everything cleanly together, and the project remains both Linux-ready and future-proof.

Health Check Endpoints

Every foundational layer we've built in this chapter, from organizing our project structure to injecting critical dependencies, serves a purpose greater than readability or testability. For the application to remain resilient and trustworthy, both humans and automation must have a reliable way to observe its condition and quickly detect issues. So here, the health check endpoints make this possible. They ensure our system is not a black box. The building of health checks directly into the App object and using injected dependencies helps to connect our architecture and operations in a unified way. Our service doesn't just run, it proves its readiness and life through transparent, standardized reporting.

Why Services need Health Checks?

Health checks aren't just useful. Instead, they're essential in the world of automated deployments, containers, and orchestration tools like Kubernetes and Docker Compose. In my mind, there are some practical motivations the Bookstore team faces:

- The orchestrators need timely, accurate signals to decide when to launch, restart, or route requests to our service.
- A lot of load balancers and managed platforms rely on endpoints to detect failures and shift traffic, avoiding downtime for users.
- The engineering team demnands quick, consistent feedback about the system's state for debugging and monitoring, not just when something goes wrong, but to prevent issues in the first place.
- As more dependencies are added (like databases, caches, external APIs), health checks keep the operational complexity manageable, failures are diagnosed early by checking each dependency, not just hoping the process responds.

Liveness vs. Readiness

Most production systems expose two kinds of health endpoints:

- "Is the process up and responding to HTTP requests?"
- "Is the service truly ready to process real user traffic?"

Both these should be as fast and lightweight as possible.

Our App struct, with injected dependencies and explicit configuration, provides the ideal place to wire up health logic. The health endpoints should not be off in some hidden file; instead, they reflect the real, current state managed by the application's top-level coordination:

```
// App struct includes DB and Logger (injected)
type App struct {
  Router *mux.Router
```

```
  DB     *sql.DB
  Logger *log.Logger
  // ...other fields
}
func (a *App) RegisterHealthEndpoints() {
  a.Router.HandleFunc("/healthz", a.LivenessHandler)
  a.Router.HandleFunc("/readyz", a.ReadinessHandler)
}
```

Checking Liveness

This handler just confirms the server is running:

```
func (a *App) LivenessHandler(w http.ResponseWriter, r
*http.Request) {
  w.Header().Set("Content-Type", "application/json")
  w.WriteHeader(http.StatusOK)
  w.Write([]byte(`{"status":"alive"}`))
}
```

Now here, what if a container platform like Kubernetes keeps regularly pinging this endpoint? If our application crashes or hangs, the check fails (non-200), triggering auto-restart so users never experience extended downtime.

Checking Readiness

Our injected database dependency lets us meaningfully assess true readiness:

```
func (a *App) ReadinessHandler(w http.ResponseWriter, r
*http.Request) {
  w.Header().Set("Content-Type", "application/json")
  if err := a.DB.Ping(); err != nil {
    a.Logger.Println("Readiness failure: DB unreachable", err)
    w.WriteHeader(http.StatusServiceUnavailable)
```

```
        w.Write([]byte(`{"status":"down","detail":"db
unreachable"}`))
        return
    }
    w.WriteHeader(http.StatusOK)
    w.Write([]byte(`{"status":"ready"}`))
}
```

The Bookstore can only serve real traffic if its primary data source is available. By running a simple ping, we avoid sending users to a broken app.

The health endpoints are not an afterthought; they are the connective tissue linking modularity, injected dependencies, and configuration. They distill the real-time health of every injected object (database, cache, logger, etc.) into a simple report, supporting automation, scaling, and recovery. As we move forward, Bookstore's operational transparency becomes a direct outgrowth of the care invested in structure, configuration, and dependency management.

CHAPTER 3: HANDLING HTTP REQUESTS AND ROUTING

This particular chapter is meant to create a pivotal stage in our Bookstore project's evolution. Where the previous chapters focused on structuring code, managing dependencies, and establishing the backbone of configuration and services, we now shift our attention to how real-world user actions traverse the internet, arrive at our application, and get turned into meaningful, reliable service. This chapter's objective is to deepen the practical knowledge of how user requests, whether a page load, a search, or a book purchase are mapped, routed, and handled by the Go's web application logic.

Here in this chapter, we will get into the Go's idioms and libraries that make the journey from HTTP request to business logic seamless and robust. The emphasis here is not only on the technical programming of routes and handlers, but on deeply understanding the "why" behind each design: how routing choices affect user experience, reliability, maintainability, and even the security of the Bookstore application.

Backbone of Web

A bustling bookstore is full of interactions, browsers, questions, orders, reviews, all happening across different aisles and counters. To support these activities, the store must have a clear layout, staff ready to guide visitors, and an effective way to connect every need to a corresponding response. In web development, this fundamental system is provided by the **HTTP protocol** and the rich set of request/response mechanics that every modern application relies on. The HTTP (HyperText Transfer Protocol) operates as the foundational backbone for communication on the World Wide Web. Every web browser, mobile app, or API client becomes a ***requester*** that talks to a server. A request is made, "Show me the fiction section," "Add this book to my cart," or "Submit my review." The server, listening on a port, must understand not only ***what*** is being asked, but ***who*** is asking and ***how*** to respond appropriately.

This request/response pattern appears deceptively simple: the client sends a request; the server interprets the request, processes any necessary logic, accesses data, and issues a response. However, each layer of this exchange is packed with information: HTTP methods (GET, POST, PUT, DELETE), headers, cookies, query strings, and sometimes even file uploads or streaming data. A robust application must decipher these signals, route them accurately, validate their contents, and return both human- and machine-friendly responses, often within milliseconds. The standard **net/http** package, without any third-party additions, provides a direct mapping from incoming HTTP requests to **handlers**, units of code designed to serve specific endpoints.

In this chapter, we will:

- Explore the anatomy of HTTP requests and responses, not just as theory but as the real framework carrying user intent to our Go server.
- Show how routes act like signposts in the store, ensuring every action finds its handler.
- Discuss the thoughtful use of HTTP verbs to mirror actions (GET to fetch, POST to

create, etc.)
- Illustrate how parameters, whether in URLs, bodies, or headers, guide feature delivery, customization, and security.

We do this not to simply wire up features, but to create a service where the Bookstore's aisles are well marked, staff (our handlers) always know what to do, and every customer journey is both traceable and improvable.

Navigate User Interactions

A bookstore exists to delight visitors, whether online or in person, by connecting their interests, questions, and purchases to the right resources. For a web application, every such connection is made by mapping user interactions to server-side routes and handlers. Imagine stepping into the Bookstore website. The landing page offers categories, search bars, and new arrivals. Each click, "Science Fiction", "Recommended for You", "Buy Book", is a purposeful signal sent from the user's browser to the Bookstore's Go server. These signals arrive as HTTP requests with unique URLs, verbs (methods), and sometimes data attached. The app's job is to interpret not only **what** is being asked, but also **who** is asking and **how** best to respond.

If we design our app's routing logic to closely follow expected user paths, we will be able to ensure that code structure actually mirrors real journeys: **`/books`** for discovering titles, **`/books/15`** to view details, **`/cart/add`** to place an order, **`/account/login`** for signing in. Every handler, our carefully crafted function, serves as the Bookstore's virtual staff, ready to meet the user's need.

From Request to Handler

As previously established in our project's architecture, the incoming requests are funneled through a central router. The router's core responsibility is to examine each request, its path, method, and potentially query parameters or headers, and direct it to the appropriate handler. The handlers themselves are designed to be clear, focused, and always aware of what the user is trying to do. Here, visiting **`/books?author=Asimov`** launches a search, sending an HTTP GET with an author parameter. The submission of a review for book 21 means sending a POST to **`/books/21/reviews`** with the review details. Similarly, resetting a forgotten password maps to **`/account/reset`**, handled by specific logic sensitive to security and validation.

So, let us consider that a user lands on the Bookstore homepage. The browser immediately sends an HTTP GET request to **/**. Here, we define a route and handler for this home page:

```
func (a *App) HomePage(w http.ResponseWriter, r *http.Request)
{

    fmt.Fprint(w, "Welcome to GitforGits Bookstore!")
```

```
}
// Router configuration
router.HandleFunc("/", app.HomePage).Methods("GET")
```

This setup ensures every visit to the root URL triggers our custom greeting.

Listing All Books

The user clicks on "All Books." The browser sends a GET request to **/books**. We wire up a handler to serve this:

```
func (a *App) ListBooks(w http.ResponseWriter, r
*http.Request) {
    books, err := a.DB.GetAllBooks()
    if err != nil {
        http.Error(w, "Could not fetch books",
http.StatusInternalServerError)
        return
    }
    w.Header().Set("Content-Type", "application/json")
    json.NewEncoder(w).Encode(books)
}
// Route
router.HandleFunc("/books", app.ListBooks).Methods("GET")
```

This not only responds to user intention but provides a machine-friendly JSON result for frontend rendering or API consumers.

Viewing Book Details

Clicking on a specific book (say, book 21) triggers a GET request to **/books/21**. The handler parses the URL parameter and delivers detail:

```
func (a *App) ShowBook(w http.ResponseWriter, r *http.Request)
{
    vars := mux.Vars(r)
    idStr := vars["id"]
```

```
    id, err := strconv.Atoi(idStr)
    if err != nil {
        http.Error(w, "Invalid ID format",
http.StatusBadRequest)
        return
    }
    book, err := a.DB.GetBookByID(id)
    if err != nil {
        http.Error(w, "Book not found", http.StatusNotFound)
        return
    }
    json.NewEncoder(w).Encode(book)
}
// Route
router.HandleFunc("/books/{id:[0-9]+}",
app.ShowBook).Methods("GET")
```

Creating a New Book (Admin)

An admin user fills a form to add a new book; this submits a POST request to **/books** with book data in the body:

```
func (a *App) CreateBook(w http.ResponseWriter, r
*http.Request) {
    var book Book
    err := json.NewDecoder(r.Body).Decode(&book)
    if err != nil {
        http.Error(w, "Invalid input", http.StatusBadRequest)
        return
    }
    err = a.DB.InsertBook(book)
    if err != nil {
```

```
        http.Error(w, "Could not add book",
http.StatusInternalServerError)
        return
    }
    w.WriteHeader(http.StatusCreated)
    json.NewEncoder(w).Encode(book)
}
// Route
router.HandleFunc("/books", app.CreateBook).Methods("POST")
```

User Search

A user filters books by author, sending a GET request to **/books?author=Asimov**:

```
func (a *App) SearchBooks(w http.ResponseWriter, r
*http.Request) {
    author := r.URL.Query().Get("author")
    books, err := a.DB.SearchBooks(author)
    if err != nil {
        http.Error(w, "Search error",
http.StatusInternalServerError)
        return
    }
    json.NewEncoder(w).Encode(books)
}
// Route
router.HandleFunc("/books", app.SearchBooks).Methods("GET")
```

(Route logic may be combined via handler code for both listing and searching.)

In all the above examples, each handler directly matches a user interaction, such as every click, form submission, or navigation action becomes a corresponding route and Go function. The pattern remains uniform: parse the request, call application logic, encode the response, and return it to the user. This mapping is central to the Bookstore's success. In the next topic, we will learn to extend our approach with more handler techniques and patterns, and further deepen your Go web development toolkit.

Handlers and HandlerFuncs

In Go, a handler is just a small piece of code that listens for a specific kind of request (like someone asking, "Where are the science fiction books?") and then gives an answer.

A Plain Function

Let's begin ultra-simple. Say you want to show an About page:

```
func AboutPage(w http.ResponseWriter, r *http.Request) {
    // This writes a simple message as the response
    fmt.Fprint(w, "Welcome to the Bookstore About Page.")
}
```

In the above,

- **`w http.ResponseWriter`** gives you a little pen to write your answer.
- **`r *http.Request`** is the letter from the visitor: their question, preferences, and sometimes data.

Now here, how do you tell Go to use this function for a certain request? So here, for this, we connect it to a specific path in your server's route map:

```
router.HandleFunc("/about", AboutPage)
```

Now, every time someone visits **`/about`**, Go runs **`AboutPage`**. Nothing more.

Accessing App Features

In a real project, the handlers need to look up books, check logins, or update orders. Instead of global variables, Go lets you attach your handler to a struct (like your app's tool kit):

```
type App struct {
    DB *sql.DB        // Your database connection
    Logger *log.Logger
}
```

Now a handler can use everything your app knows:

```
func (a *App) ListBooks(w http.ResponseWriter, r
*http.Request) {
    // Grab the list of books from the DB—not just a message
    books := []string{"Dune", "Foundation", "Go Programming in
Action"}
    json.NewEncoder(w).Encode(books)
}
```

We then attach this like so:

```
router.HandleFunc("/books", app.ListBooks)
```

You only need a Handler (with extra struct/state) if a particular path has special resources to keep track of. Most of the time, you'll write a regular function; if your feature needs something extra (like a database connection), you'll write a method attached to your app's main struct.

Explore Routes

It's like when you're in a bookstore and you start in the Home section, then move to the Fiction section, then the Cart, and the system keeps track of the path you take. Routes are like the detailed map that guides every HTTP request to the right place in your code, making sure every feature is accessible, easy to find, and reliable.

Understanding Routes

The routes connect the "outside" (user clicks, browser requests) to the "inside" (custom logic, database queries, personalized responses) without confusion. They allow you to organize your website's paths so users always find what they're looking for and your code never gets tangled.

For example, let us think of a simple route for your Bookstore's homepage:

```
func HomePage(w http.ResponseWriter, r *http.Request) {
    fmt.Fprint(w, "Welcome to Bookstore Home!")
}
router.HandleFunc("/", HomePage)
```

Now here, when someone visits `/`, Go runs **`HomePage`**. No matter how big your project grows, this route stays clear and focused.

Static vs. Dynamic Routes

The static routes are like fixed signs. They are always pointing to the same content:

```
router.HandleFunc("/about", AboutPage)
router.HandleFunc("/contact", ContactPage)
```

And, the dynamic routes, however, have built-in flexibility. They allow you to handle specific items, like a particular book:

```
router.HandleFunc("/books/{id}", ShowBook)
```

So here, let us consider that the Bookstore has a hundred books. You don't need a hundred separate handlers. Just one route handles them all, and your code reads the ID from the URL to see which book to show.

Working with HTTP Methods

The routes don't just match paths; they decide what kind of action to run with different HTTP verbs:

- GET asks for information
- POST submits new data
- PUT updates existing records
- DELETE removes something

For example, for **`/books`**:

- Show all books:

```
router.HandleFunc("/books", ListBooks).Methods("GET")
```

- Create a new book:

```
router.HandleFunc("/books", CreateBook).Methods("POST")
```

- Update:

```
router.HandleFunc("/books/{id}", UpdateBook).Methods("PUT")
```

- Delete:

```
router.HandleFunc("/books/{id}", DeleteBook).Methods("DELETE")
```

All the routes, handlers, and methods are like shelves or counters in a bookstore, ready for any visitor.

Wildcards and Route Prefixes

Sometimes, you want a sign that covers a whole area, not just one shelf:

```
router.PathPrefix("/assets/").Handler(http.StripPrefix("/asset
s/", http.FileServer(http.Dir("./web/assets/"))))
```

Anything under **`/assets/`**, images, JavaScript, styles, goes through the file server, saving you from writing dozens of similar routes.

Suppose you want a Bookstore where users can:

- See the homepage (/)
- Browse all books (**`/books`**)
- View a single book (**`/books/12`**)
- Add a new book (**`/books`** with POST)
- Remove a book (**`/books/12`** with DELETE)

So here, your routes look like this in code:

```
router.HandleFunc("/", HomePage)

router.HandleFunc("/books", ListBooks).Methods("GET")

router.HandleFunc("/books", CreateBook).Methods("POST")

router.HandleFunc("/books/{id}", ShowBook).Methods("GET")

router.HandleFunc("/books/{id}", DeleteBook).Methods("DELETE")
```

Now, any user action matches the right handler naturally. The feeling is just like moving from aisle to aisle with clear signs overhead. There are no lost visitors, no mysterious errors. The well-designed routes give confidence to users (intuitive URLs), resilience to code (easy updates), and power to developers (simple expansion and testing).

URL Parameters

We now move on to the URL parameters. These are the blank spaces on your Bookstore's signs. These are spaces you can fill in with any detail, like a specific book's number or a search term. They let a single route handle dozens, hundreds, or infinite possibilities, all while keeping your code simple and maintainable.

Without parameters, you'd need a new route for every book or category… clearly not practical. Parameters let the app "listen" for changing inputs and respond in dynamic, personalized ways.

Path Parameters

Suppose a user clicks on a book titled "Go in Practice," which has the ID 7. They're sent to **/books/7**. The **{id}** section of your route catches this number:

```
router.HandleFunc("/books/{id}", ShowBook)
```

Now here, how does your code get the value?

So for this, inside your handler:

```
func ShowBook(w http.ResponseWriter, r *http.Request) {
    vars := mux.Vars(r)            // Pulls all path variables
    bookID := vars["id"]           // Gets the value of {id}
    fmt.Fprintf(w, "Book ID: %s", bookID)
}
```

This means **/books/12** and **/books/99** both hit the same handler, and your code gets the right number every time.

Query Parameters

Sometimes, users want to filter or search, not just see a single resource. They might visit **/books?author=asimov&page=2**. That stuff after the **?** is the query parameters, key-value pairs you can pull out of the request easily.

Following is how we do it:

```
func SearchBooks(w http.ResponseWriter, r *http.Request) {
    author := r.URL.Query().Get("author")
    page := r.URL.Query().Get("page")
    fmt.Fprintf(w, "Author: %s, Page: %s", author, page)
}
```

You can define your route for all such searches simply:

```
router.HandleFunc("/books", SearchBooks) // Handles all GET /books?.....
```

Combining Path and Query Parameters

Let's say, we want the reviews live at **/books/14/reviews?page=3**:

```
router.HandleFunc("/books/{id}/reviews", BookReviews)
```

And retrieve both:

```
func BookReviews(w http.ResponseWriter, r *http.Request) {
    vars := mux.Vars(r)
    bookID := vars["id"]
    page := r.URL.Query().Get("page")
    fmt.Fprintf(w, "Reviews for book %s on page %s", bookID, page)
}
```

Now, the URL structure is both readable and practical, and your code adjusts to the exact need.

Grouping Routes

There are experiences that, with features like book browsing, reviews, user profiles, admin tools, and orders, the sheer number of routes quickly becomes unwieldy. And, if every path is defined separately, your code will become tangled, harder to secure, and difficult for others (or even yourself) to navigate. So here, the concept of grouping routes works better. It is a strategy borrowed from real bookstores, wherein we by organizing related topics together on shelves, you make browsing intuitive, maintenance manageable, and policy application (like authentication) efficient.

What "Grouping Routes" Mean?

Grouping routes means bundling together all endpoints that share a common base path or logical function. This way, routes with similar responsibilities, like all those that manage books, or all those that deal with users, reside together, not scattered across the app. It's like declaring, "Everything under **/books** is about book operations, everything under **/admin** is for admin staff."

The Go's **gorilla/mux** router brings this to life using subrouters, tools specifically designed to help you organize and manage your app's structure as it grows.

Bringing Order with Subrouters

Let's see how this works in practice. We can think that we want all book-related features under a unified area:

```
booksRouter := router.PathPrefix("/books").Subrouter()

booksRouter.HandleFunc("", app.ListBooks).Methods("GET")
// GET /books

booksRouter.HandleFunc("", app.CreateBook).Methods("POST")
// POST /books

booksRouter.HandleFunc("/{id:[0-9]+}",
app.ShowBook).Methods("GET") // GET /books/12

booksRouter.HandleFunc("/{id:[0-9]+}/reviews",
app.GetReviews).Methods("GET")
```

Now here, you can notice how every book task, from listing to reviews, stays under **/books**. You don't repeat yourself with **/books** everywhere, just set it once and define the actions inside the group.

Middleware as a First-Class Routing Concept

Can you imagine every request to your bookstore takes a short trip through a bunch of checkpoints even before it hits your main handler? Each checkpoint can record what's happening, verify the user, limit access speed, or transform data. These checkpoints are called middleware: simple, reusable bits of code that "wrap around" your handlers. Middleware makes sure every request is processed securely, efficiently, and in a consistent way.

With middleware, you can separate things like logging, error handling, and user authentication from the business logic. This helps avoid repeating code in every handler, keeping the app's core functions cleaner and easier to maintain.

What Middleware look like?

A middleware is just a function that takes a **http.Handler** (your handler or another middleware), does something, and then calls the next handler in the chain. The pattern is simple but powerful:

```
func LoggingMiddleware(next http.Handler) http.Handler {
```

```
    return http.HandlerFunc(func(w http.ResponseWriter, r
*http.Request) {
        log.Printf("%s %s", r.Method, r.URL.Path)
        next.ServeHTTP(w, r) // Pass control to the next
handler
    })
}
```

Here, every incoming request is logged before passing control onward.

Attaching Middleware to Routes/Groups

The Gorilla Mux lets you attach middleware to:

- Every route (global)
- One route group (like **`/admin`**)
- Even a single handler for special cases

Following is how you attach it:

```
router.Use(LoggingMiddleware)
```

Every route now logs each request.

Similarly, for a group-specific:

```
adminRouter := router.PathPrefix("/admin").Subrouter()
adminRouter.Use(AdminAuth) // Only admin routes require admin
check
```

And, for a single route:

```
router.Handle("/settings", RateLimit(SettingsHandler))
```

Middleware is more than just a tool. It's a way to design your bookstore so that each request is handled safely, efficiently, and with maximum flexibility, all without cluttering up your code.

Navigate Web Routing with Gorilla/Mux

Now that you've seen the basics, we now go deeper into our understanding and make use of Gorilla Mux's full power to create a Bookstore web app that's both intuitive for users and easy for developers to maintain.

Combining Route Patterns

You can use the same route for different actions, like showing, updating, and deleting books, but they respond to different HTTP methods.

```
router.HandleFunc("/books/{id:[0-9]+}",
ShowBook).Methods("GET")

router.HandleFunc("/books/{id:[0-9]+}",
UpdateBook).Methods("PUT")

router.HandleFunc("/books/{id:[0-9]+}",
DeleteBook).Methods("DELETE")
```

This ties together all lifecycle actions for a single resource in one neat pattern.

Grouping Feature Areas with Subrouters

The more your bookstore grows, the more important it is to keep the code for books, users, orders, and admin tasks separate.

Here's the lowdown on the Books Group:

```
books := router.PathPrefix("/books").Subrouter()

books.HandleFunc("", ListBooks).Methods("GET")

books.HandleFunc("", CreateBook).Methods("POST")

books.HandleFunc("/{id:[0-9]+}", ShowBook).Methods("GET")

books.HandleFunc("/{id:[0-9]+}/reviews",
GetReviews).Methods("GET")

books.HandleFunc("/{id:[0-9]+}/reviews",
AddReview).Methods("POST")
```

This one is for the User Group:

```
users := router.PathPrefix("/users").Subrouter()

users.HandleFunc("/register", RegisterUser).Methods("POST")

users.HandleFunc("/login", LoginUser).Methods("POST")
```

And, this is for the Admin Group:

```
admin := router.PathPrefix("/admin").Subrouter()
```

```
admin.HandleFunc("/dashboard", AdminDashboard).Methods("GET")
admin.HandleFunc("/stats", ShowStats).Methods("GET")
admin.Use(AdminAuthMiddleware)
```

Each group can have its own middleware, such as authentication, logging, or rate limiting.

Schemes, Hosts, Headers, and Queries

We can also do the match based on more than just the URL:

- Scheme (force HTTPS):

```
router.HandleFunc("/settings",
SecureSettings).Schemes("https")
```

- Host (multi-tenancy or subdomains):

```
router.Host("admin.bookstore.com").HandleFunc("/dashboard",
AdminDashboard)
```

- Headers:

```
router.HandleFunc("/api", ApiHandler).Headers("X-Bookstore-
Auth", "super-secret")
```

- Queries:

```
router.HandleFunc("/search", SearchBooks).Queries("author",
"{author:[a-zA-Z]+}")
```

Gorilla Mux keeps your bookstore's routes on par with those expertly marked shelves you find in a well-kept library. It helps users find what they need quickly, staff (developers) can easily add new sections or services, and everyone enjoys a smooth browse, even as the store grows or routines evolve.

Error Handling in Go

Imagine a customer in your Bookstore asks for a book that isn't in stock, the shopkeeper doesn't just shrug and walk away. He explains, maybe offers alternatives, or says when the book will be available. Likewise, a well-designed web app should treat errors not as collapses, but as opportunities to guide users, keep them informed, and aid developers in fixing problems swiftly.

Responding to Errors

Suppose someone tries to look up book 321, but your database only has books up to 300. Following is going to be a classic handler, written with Mux:

```
func ShowBook(w http.ResponseWriter, r *http.Request) {
    vars := mux.Vars(r)
    id := vars["id"]
    book, err := db.FindBook(id)
    if err != nil {
        http.Error(w, "Book Not Found", http.StatusNotFound)
        return
    }
    json.NewEncoder(w).Encode(book)
}
```

So here,

- If **`db.FindBook(id)`** returns an error, the server sends a 404 (not found) with a helpful message.
- Otherwise, the book's data is returned.

Fixing Issues

So here, we need to always log the details server-side, even if you don't show them to regular users:

```
func CreateBook(w http.ResponseWriter, r *http.Request) {
    var book Book
    err := json.NewDecoder(r.Body).Decode(&book)
    if err != nil {
        log.Printf("[CreateBook] Failed to decode input: %v",
err)
        http.Error(w, "Invalid book data format",
http.StatusBadRequest)
        return
```

```
    }
    // further logic here...
}
```

In the above,

- Logs help you trace back problems quickly.
- Users only see actionable feedback (like "Check your form input").

Custom Error Pages

Now there are cases, wherein not every route will exist, and not every action will succeed. So here, the Go/Mux lets you assign a custom error handler for routes that don't match:

```
router.NotFoundHandler = http.HandlerFunc(func(w
http.ResponseWriter, r *http.Request) {
    http.Error(w, "Sorry, that page does not exist in our
Bookstore.", http.StatusNotFound)
})
```

For APIs, a friendly JSON message might look like:

```
func ApiError(w http.ResponseWriter, code int, message string)
{
    w.Header().Set("Content-Type", "application/json")
    w.WriteHeader(code)
    json.NewEncoder(w).Encode(map[string]string{"error":
message})
}
```

This is used for validation failures or internal server errors. A good error handling means your Bookstore never feels broken. It feels responsive, informative, and easy to trust. For developers and maintainers, it turns confusion into clarity.

Rate Limiting and Request Throttling

So, picture this. Suddenly, your bookstore is slammed with thousands of visitors. Some are there to buy, some are just browsing, and, let's be real, some are bots trying to crash your site. To stay reliable and fair, you need a way to make sure one visitor (or a small group) can't hog all the website's capacity.

You've got rate limiting and request throttling to keep things safe. They keep an eye on traffic, politely slow down requests that come up again, and block bursts that would otherwise mess up your flow.

How Rate Limiting Works?

In Go, rate limiting is often added as middleware, watchers that check every request before passing it along. Following is a pattern for a rate-limiting middleware using the popular **tollbooth** library, wrapped into a function:

```
import "github.com/didip/tollbooth"

func RateLimiter(next http.Handler) http.Handler {

    limiter := tollbooth.NewLimiter(10, nil) // 10 requests per second

    return http.HandlerFunc(func(w http.ResponseWriter, r *http.Request) {

        err := tollbooth.LimitByRequest(limiter, w, r)

        if err != nil {

            http.Error(w, err.Error(), http.StatusTooManyRequests)

            return

        }

        next.ServeHTTP(w, r)

    })

}
```

Now, attach it globally or to just one route/group:

```
router.Use(RateLimiter) // All requests limited

books.Use(RateLimiter) // Only book endpoints limited
```

Throttling for Sensitive Actions

Suppose you don't want users to hammer the "Add to Cart" button:

```
cart := router.PathPrefix("/cart").Subrouter()
cart.Use(RateLimiter)
cart.HandleFunc("/add", AddToCart).Methods("POST")
```

Now, even if a bot tries to overload the checkout, your Bookstore keeps its cool.

Throttling for Public APIs

When exposing an endpoint (like **`/api/v1/books`**) to outside developers or partners, use higher-level throttling or authentication-based limits so that one integration partner can't exhaust resources:

```
api := router.PathPrefix("/api").Subrouter()
api.Use(ApiKeyRateLimiter)
api.HandleFunc("/v1/books", ApiBooks).Methods("GET")
```

With proper rate limiting and request throttling, your Bookstore won't just survive popularity, it'll thrive, keeping every visitor happy (and every developer sane).

Performing CRUD Operations

The true test of any web app is how well it lets users (and other systems) create, read, update, and delete. For a bookstore, this means handling the life cycle of books: adding new books to your inventory, listing what's available, updating details (like price or stock), and removing books as needed. CRUD handlers that are designed well are key to any RESTful web service.

Adding a New Book

When a user or admin submits a form (or frontend sends a POST request) to **`/books`**, they're asking you to create a new book in the Bookstore:

```
func CreateBook(w http.ResponseWriter, r *http.Request) {
    var book Book
    err := json.NewDecoder(r.Body).Decode(&book)
    if err != nil {
        http.Error(w, "Invalid book data",
http.StatusBadRequest)
        return
```

```
    }
    // Assume db.InsertBook adds the book and sets its ID
    err = db.InsertBook(&book)
    if err != nil {
        http.Error(w, "Could not save book",
http.StatusInternalServerError)
        return
    }
    w.WriteHeader(http.StatusCreated)
    json.NewEncoder(w).Encode(book)
}
```

Listing and Showing Books

- List All Books

```
func ListBooks(w http.ResponseWriter, r *http.Request) {
    books, err := db.GetAllBooks()
    if err != nil {
        http.Error(w, "Could not retrieve books",
http.StatusInternalServerError)
        return
    }
    json.NewEncoder(w).Encode(books)
}
```

- Show One Book

```
func ShowBook(w http.ResponseWriter, r *http.Request) {
    vars := mux.Vars(r)
    id := vars["id"]
    book, err := db.FindBook(id)
    if err != nil {
```

```
        http.Error(w, "Book not found", http.StatusNotFound)
        return
    }
    json.NewEncoder(w).Encode(book)
}
```

Modifying Existing Books

Suppose you want to edit a book's details:

```
func UpdateBook(w http.ResponseWriter, r *http.Request) {
    vars := mux.Vars(r)
    id := vars["id"]
    var book Book
    err := json.NewDecoder(r.Body).Decode(&book)
    if err != nil {
        http.Error(w, "Invalid input", http.StatusBadRequest)
        return
    }
    err = db.UpdateBook(id, &book)
    if err != nil {
        http.Error(w, "Could not update book",
http.StatusInternalServerError)
        return
    }
    json.NewEncoder(w).Encode(book)
}
```

Removing a Book

```
func DeleteBook(w http.ResponseWriter, r *http.Request) {
    vars := mux.Vars(r)
```

```
    id := vars["id"]
    err := db.DeleteBook(id)
    if err != nil {
        http.Error(w, "Could not delete book",
http.StatusInternalServerError)
        return
    }
    w.WriteHeader(http.StatusNoContent) // Success, no body
needed
}
```

All these CRUD handlers follow the RESTful patterns introduced earlier, and by pairing them with well-designed routes using Gorilla Mux, your code remains clean and easy to grow. Each HTTP method, route, and handler is mapped to a clear intent: add, show, modify, or remove resources, and every response, good or bad, comes with a helpful status code and message.

Summary

To sum it up, we learned how a web app like the Bookstore mapped user actions to robust server logic using Go's powerful routing and handler patterns. The HTTP requests were broken down to show what each user wanted to do, and Gorilla Mux was used to make flexible, expressive routes and organize them using subrouters for clean code. We figured out how handlers, from simple functions to struct-based methods, connected routes to business logic, and then got the hang of extracting dynamic and query parameters to personalize responses.

And, we explored the concepts of error handling by showing how thoughtful feedback and precise status codes improved both user experience and developer debugging. All these patterns were tied together by the CRUD operation walkthrough, which offered hands-on examples for creating, reading, updating, and deleting real bookstore resources. And by the time we finished this chapter, we had a practical toolkit for designing, scaling, and maintaining web features that intelligently respond to every user request.

Chapter 4: Templating and Rendering Content

Welcome to the next chapter 4! We've already gone over how the user interactions are routed, handled, and stored in the Bookstore app. In this chapter, we're going to look at how those responses turn into beautiful, dynamic web pages, and how Go takes data and turns it into HTML that real users can see. Mastering template rendering is key for any production web app. With it, you can build layouts that can adapt to different situations, fill pages with live catalog data, display custom error messages, and collect customer input through forms. And the best part is that you can do all of this while keeping the code manageable and secure.

By the end of this chapter, you'll know how to:

- Use Go's powerful templating engine to inject data into your web pages
- Compose modular layouts with nested templates for consistent navigation, headers, and footers
- Build dynamic home, catalog, and detail views for the Bookstore
- Design and process HTML forms for features like login, registration, and reviews
- Optimize performance with template caching and mitigate security risks with safe rendering
- Debug template errors quickly and handle tricky cases with confidence

Throughout the chapter, we'll illustrate every step with real Bookstore code and scenarios, from showing personalized greetings and sale banners, to rendering nested book lists and order summaries. The skills in this chapter will make your app adaptable, good-looking, and robust for both users and future developers.

Dynamic Rendering Overview

The concept of dynamic rendering refers to the process where the server generates HTML pages on-the-fly by merging predefined templates with real-time data. It contrasts with static sites, which serve fixed HTML regardless of context. It enables your Bookstore to deliver personalized and up-to-date content, such as the latest book listings, user-specific recommendations, shopping cart details, and up-to-the-minute sales or events.

The dynamic rendering involves templates, files containing HTML mixed with placeholders and simple logic, and the code that fills these placeholders with data during each request. When a user requests a page, your Go server executes the handler associated with that route, which collects the relevant data (e.g., book details, user info), injects it into the appropriate template, and sends the resulting fully-formed HTML back to the user's browser.

This process offers several crucial advantages for our Bookstore application:

- Different users can see customized content tailored to their preferences or status (like logged-in greetings).
- The content reflects the latest inventory, prices, reviews, or deals.
- Templates separate presentation (HTML structure and look) from business logic (data and processing), allowing designers and developers to work more independently.

- The **html/template** package automatically escapes content, preventing common web vulnerabilities such as cross-site scripting (XSS).
- Components like headers, footers, and navigation bars can be modularized and reused across multiple pages.

The Go's **html/template** is uniquely suited for dynamic rendering because it blends performance with safety and flexibility. Unlike string concatenation or embedding HTML within code, templates are parsed once and executed efficiently for every request. The Go standard library provides familiar control structures (loops, conditionals), secure handling of user content, and straightforward ways to pass complex data.

As we continuye to explore this chapter, you will learn to build on these ideas, first diving into basic template syntax, then progressing towards nested templates, handling user inputs via forms, optimizing template caching to improve speed, safe HTML rendering, and finally troubleshooting common template errors.

Templates Deep Dive

The Templates are Go's way of separating how data looks from how it gets processed. Instead of writing HTML inside your code, you put HTML (with special placeholders and logic) into dedicated template files. Your Go handlers then fill in those placeholders with real values, book titles, prices, user names, and the templates output the finished pages.

Basics: Variables and Placeholders

The template files use **{{ ... }}** to embed data. For example:

```
<h1>{{ .Title }}</h1>
<p>{{ .Description }}</p>
```

Here, the **.Title** and **.Description** refer to fields on a struct or map you pass to the template. When you load the Bookstore homepage, the handler populates these fields (maybe with today's featured book).

Lists and Loops

To list books or reviews, the templates give you loops:

```
<ul>
{{ range .Books }}
  <li>{{ .Title }} – ${{ .Price }}</li>
```

```
{{ end }}
</ul>
```

If you pass a slice of books, every item is shown. The empty slices simply render nothing.

Conditional Logic

The templates can show or hide sections using **`if`**:

```
{{ if .OnSale }}
  <div class="sale-banner">SALE!</div>
{{ end }}
```

Or, can also handle the missing data:

```
{{ if .Reviews }}
  <h3>Reviews:</h3>
  {{ range .Reviews }}
    <div>{{ .Text }}</div>
  {{ end }}
{{ else }}
  <p>No reviews yet.</p>
{{ end }}
```

Functions and Pipelines

The templates can run basic formatting functions using the pipe symbol **|**:

```
<p>{{ .Price | printf "$%.2f" }}</p>
```

We can also register custom functions, like formatting dates or capitalizing text, and make them available in your templates.

Rendering Templates in Handlers

A Bookstore handler typically looks like this:

```
func ShowBook(w http.ResponseWriter, r *http.Request) {
```

```
    book := Book{Title: "Go in Action", Price: 19.99, OnSale: true}
    tmpl := template.Must(template.ParseFiles("templates/book.html"))
    tmpl.Execute(w, book)
}
```

In practice, you'll cache parsed templates for speed (covered later), but the core idea is always: load, fill, output.

Nested Templates in Action

As our Bookstore project grows, we notice that every page starts sharing common elements, a header with navigation links, a footer with copyright info, perhaps a cart preview or search bar. Now here, rather than rewriting the same HTML in every template, we use nested templates so our site remains organized, consistent, and easy to expand.

We then work together to set up main layouts and modular components. Let us think of it as puzzle pieces:

- **`base.html`** sets out the overall structure of every page.
- **`header.html`** shows the shop name, navigation, and maybe even a search box.
- **`footer.html`** wraps things up with links and credits.
- **`booklist.html`** displays a collection of books.
- **`book.html`** offers details for a single book.

We embed these smaller pieces into our master layout using Go's **`{{ template "name" . }}`** syntax. So here, in the below, our base layout may look like:

```
<html>
  <body>
    {{ template "header" . }}
    <main>
      {{ block "content" . }}{{ end }}
    </main>
    {{ template "footer" . }}
  </body>
</html>
```

Next, inside **booklist.html**, we define a block for main content:

```
{{ define "content" }}
  <h1>Available Books</h1>
  <ul>
    {{ range .Books }}
      <li>{{ .Title }} by {{ .Author }}</li>
    {{ end }}
  </ul>
{{ end }}
```

In our primary Go code, we then load and combine these templates:

```
tmpl := template.Must(template.ParseFiles(
    "templates/base.html",
    "templates/header.html",
    "templates/footer.html",
    "templates/booklist.html",
))
tmpl.ExecuteTemplate(w, "base", pageData)
```

When we structure our templates like this, we make sure that updates to the header or footer show up right away on every page. We use nested templates to keep our Bookstore fresh and DRY. We don't have to worry about duplicating the layout, and we can make future changes, like branding, promotions, or seasonal themes, without stressing out.

Next, we'll design our main page layout, putting these template pieces together for a polished, inviting visitor experience.

Design Main Page Layout

We commonly know that the homepage is often the first thing users see, so it needs to communicate the value of our store, showcase the latest and greatest books, and make core actions like searching, browsing, and logging in accessible.

We begin by sketching the overall structure our homepage should follow. Typically, this means dividing the page into distinct sections that work together:

- A **persistent header** that contains the bookstore name and navigation links to major sections (Home, Categories, Cart, Login). Having these at the top means users never get lost. We also usually include a search bar here, so readers can find their favorite titles from any page.
- There is **Banner or Hero zone** where we spotlight a promotion, announce a new arrival, or greet logged-in users by name. We might conditionally show a message ("Spring Sale! 15% off all fiction books!") using template logic like:

```
{{ if .Banner }}
  <div class="banner">{{ .Banner }}</div>
{{ end }}
```

- We also have **flash messages** which are the short feedback notes you see after actions (like "Review added!" or "Login failed"). We can render them only when present:

```
{{ if .Flash }}
  <div class="flash">{{ .Flash }}</div>
{{ end }}
```

These tiny messages are vital for friendly UX, especially as users register or check out.

- There are **category links or sidebar** for larger stores. Here, we may show major categories or genre filters, allowing users to jump directly to the books they care about.
- Then, there is **main content block** where the action happens. It shows featured books, bestseller lists, personalized suggestions, recent reviews, or new arrivals. We design this block to use nested templates so we swap out what's displayed without touching the page layout.

For instance, to loop through featured books:

```
{{ define "content" }}
  <h2>Featured Books</h2>
  <ul>
    {{ range .FeaturedBooks }}
      <li>
        <a href="/books/{{ .ID }}">{{ .Title }}</a>
        by {{ .Author }} - ${{ .Price }}
      </li>
```

```
    {{ end }}
  </ul>
{{ end }}
```

- We also have **footer** which anchors our page, providing copyright, contact info, and extra navigation. It's usually included in all templates via nesting.

```
<footer>
  <p>&copy; 2025 GitforGits Bookstore. All rights reserved.</p>
  <nav>
    <a href="/about">About Us</a>
    <a href="/privacy">Privacy Policy</a>
  </nav>
</footer>
```

So now, als learned previously, we will make use of the nested templates to combine these pieces for every page:

```
// Load all fragments and base layout in one call
tmpl := template.Must(template.ParseFiles(
    "templates/base.html",
    "templates/header.html",
    "templates/footer.html",
    "templates/maincontent.html",
))
tmpl.ExecuteTemplate(w, "base", homepageData)
```

By working this way, we get consistent structure across the site (every page gets header, footer, flash message slots). It gives us the ability to update navigation or site layout by editing one template. This technical structure (using blocks, ranges, conditionals) lets us keep the site adaptable and fresh, all while making sure future changes don't mean tedious work or inconsistent style.

Handling Forms and User Inputs

We're not just about showing our customers what we've got, it's about collecting interactions. We help users do all sorts of things, like signing up, logging in, searching for books, reviewing purchases, and checking out orders. What this means is that we need to build forms in our templates, that is, spaces for users to enter data, and write server code to process, validate, and securely store that input.

Form Creation

We start with simple HTML forms. For registration, our template may look like:

```
<form action="/register" method="POST">
  <label for="username">Username:</label>
  <input type="text" id="username" name="username">

  <label for="password">Password:</label>
  <input type="password" id="password" name="password">

  <button type="submit">Register</button>
</form>
```

If we want to enable book reviews, we create a review form:

```
<form action="/books/{{ .ID }}/review" method="POST">
  <label for="review">Your Review:</label>
  <textarea id="review" name="review"></textarea>
  <button type="submit">Submit</button>
</form>
```

We use template placeholders (like **`{{ .ID }}`**) so forms know which resource they are for, making them dynamic and context-aware.

Capturing and Processing Input

In our Go handlers, we read values from form fields using the **`r.FormValue`** method:

```
func RegisterUser(w http.ResponseWriter, r *http.Request) {
    // Make sure method is POST
```

```
    if r.Method != http.MethodPost {
        http.Error(w, "Method Not Allowed",
http.StatusMethodNotAllowed)
        return
    }
    username := r.FormValue("username")
    password := r.FormValue("password")
    // Validate, sanitize, save, give feedback!
}
```

This pattern also works for search forms:

```
func SearchBooks(w http.ResponseWriter, r *http.Request) {
    query := r.FormValue("q")
    // Fetch books matching 'query', show results
}
```

Validation and Security

We never trust direct user input. We validate (check length, format), sanitize (strip unwanted characters), and always escape user data before displaying it:

- For login, we check if the credentials are well-formed.
- For reviews, we avoid empty or abusive submissions.

When errors happen, we return the form with explanatory messages using template placeholders:

```
{{ if .Error }}
  <div class="error">{{ .Error }}</div>
{{ end }}
```

Redirects and Reusability

After successful actions, we often redirect users or show confirmation:

```
http.Redirect(w, r, "/welcome", http.StatusSeeOther)
```

Or pass the flash messages using session values for feedback on the page.

We also build forms as template fragments, login, register, checkout, keeping them separate for easy reuse and customization. These fragments can be nested into main pages or pop-ups, as our Bookstore UX evolves.

Next, we'll optimize page load times and server performance by implementing template caching to avoid unnecessary parsing and improve responsiveness as our app grows.

Template Caching

Depending on the page, you might need to load, parse, and merge a bunch of templates with data. If we reload and reparse our templates every single request, our server works much harder than necessary, wasting CPU and slowing response times. That's why we set up template caching. It parses each template once at startup and uses the compiled version for every user visit.

Why Cache Templates?

When we parse a template file (like **`template.ParseFiles(...)`**), the Go converts the HTML and template logic into an internal form ready for execution. But this is expensive. Instead, we can:

- Parse all our templates into a map or struct once, when our server starts
- Store the ready-to-use template objects in memory
- Retrieve them instantly for each incoming request

Setting up Template Cache

Since you have understood the concept of template caching, we now build a simple cache at app startup:

```
// At server boot:

var templates =
template.Must(template.ParseGlob("templates/*.html"))

// In every handler:

func HomePage(w http.ResponseWriter, r *http.Request) {

    pageData := ... // fill with homepage info

    err := templates.ExecuteTemplate(w, "base", pageData)

    if err != nil {

        log.Printf("Template error: %v", err)
```

```
        http.Error(w, "Internal error",
http.StatusInternalServerError)
    }
}
```

For a bit more control, we might use a map:

```
var templateCache = map[string]*template.Template{}
func init() {
    files := []string{"base.html", "header.html",
"footer.html", "maincontent.html"}
    for _, name := range files {
        tmpl := template.Must(template.ParseFiles("templates/"
+ name))
        templateCache[name] = tmpl
    }
}
```

Then in handlers:

```
tmpl := templateCache["maincontent.html"]
tmpl.ExecuteTemplate(w, "base", pageData)
```

Doing this, we gain the benfit of:

- No repeated parsing, hence lower latency for every request.
- Faster page loads for users, even under high traffic.
- Cleaner error handling: any template bugs are caught at startup, not during a live request.

So, when we update our site's design, we simply restart our server to reload templates. For production-grade Bookstore apps, the template caching is a must for performance, scalability, and operational safety.

Safe HTML Rendering

Now, this safe html rendering is also very important concept. Here, we keep user content and our Bookstore secure from cross-site scripting attacks and unexpected HTML injection.

When we build interactive sites, the users get to contribute data: book reviews, usernames, even search terms. If we're not careful, these user inputs can introduce risky HTML or scripts that, if rendered raw, could compromise our site and our users, classic cross-site scripting (XSS) attacks. This concept is meant to always treat user content as untrusted and escaping it automatically before it's blended into a template.

How Go's html/template Secures?

Well, the good news is, that the **html/template** package handles escaping for us. Whenever we use **{{ .Field }}** in templates, the Go converts unsafe characters, like **<**, **>**, and **&**, into safe HTML entities so browser never runs unwanted code.

Let us say that if someone enters **<script>alert("XSS!")</script>** as a book review, and we render:

```
<div>{{ .Review }}</div>
```

The Go automatically shows:

```
<div>&lt;script&gt;alert("XSS!")&lt;/script&gt;</div>
```

So here, no malicious code is executed; our users stay safe.

Sometimes, we need to output HTML, like a review containing bolded text. For these scenarios, the Go offers **template.HTML**:

```
type Review struct {
    Text template.HTML // we manually mark this as safe
}
```

We must be very careful here. We need to use only the **template.HTML** for content you trust or have fully sanitized.

Template Debugging

Sometimes, we run into situations where something isn't displaying as we expected. You might see that a book list is empty, there's no error message, or the Go server prints a template error in the console. We use debugging templates in our development workflow, just like we use reviewing logs or checking function outputs.

So, let's walk through a scenario. It's a homepage that's supposed to show featured books, but none are showing up.

Diagnosing Missing Data

As we build out the Bookstore's homepage, we often want to show lists like featured books. If nothing appears, we can add a fallback to our template:

```
<ul>
  {{ range .FeaturedBooks }}
    <li>{{ .Title }}</li>
  {{ else }}
    <li>No featured books available.</li>
  {{ end }}
</ul>
```

This makes it clear whether our data is truly present or not. If the fallback displays, our handler needs attention.

Inside our Go code, we then add a logging statement to see what gets sent to the template:

```
log.Printf("FeaturedBooks: %+v", pageData.FeaturedBooks)
```

If we notice the slice is empty, we investigate our database query or data assignment. Fixing the handler ensures the next page load has real book content.

Debugging Error Messages and Logic

Suppose our template expects an error block after a failed form submission:

```
{{ if .Error }}
  <div class="error">{{ .Error }}</div>
{{ end }}
```

When nothing shows up, we check our Go struct and verify the field is set:

```
data := PageData{Error: "Username already exists"}
```

Ensuring the field name matches and is always set resolves most display issues.

If Go prints a template error like "unexpected '}'", we open the relevant file, check block starts (`{{if ...}}`, `{{range ...}}`), and ensure all blocks are really closed (`{{end}}`). If we fix the syntax quickly, it restores the page rendering.

Summary

So, we took a look at how Go's template system lets you do dynamic rendering in the Bookstore app, giving every page the latest, personalized content. We also learned to create HTML templates with variables, loops, conditionals, and blocks, making sure presentation and application data were separated. We made templates for headers, footers, and main content that fit together so the site layout stays consistent, but can adapt to different page needs. We made some changes to improve application performance, like implementing template caching. This made sure that templates were only parsed once for fast server responses with each request. We used Go's automatic HTML escaping to keep our web pages safe, learning to trust content and prevent cross-site scripting.

We've worked through all these challenges together, and it's given us the skills to build secure, flexible, and visually consistent web pages for any feature our Bookstore needs.

Chapter 5: Interaction with Databases

Over the period, one recognizes that the reliable storage is essential for everything from user accounts and orders to reviews and inventory. This chapter will guide us in understanding how to design and interact with databases, keeping every customer, catalog entry, and transaction safe and accessible between visits. We'll see not just the theoretical reasons for using persistent storage, but hands-on strategies for modelling data, executing database operations, enforcing integrity, optimizing performance, and scaling our system. This chapter will make us capable to choose and design database schemas that fit our needs, connect and query them using Go's tools, and put our knowledge into practice with real-world Bookstore scenarios.

Why Persistent Storage Matters?

When you're making any kind of web applicaton, especially something as interactive and feature-rich as our Bookstore, you've really got to think about persistent storage. It's not just an option, it's fundamental. With persistent storage, data gets written somewhere durable, like a disk or a database, so it stays intact even if the application restarts, a server crashes, or users come and go. If there's no persistent storage, all the work that users do, like registering accounts, buying books and submitting reviews, would be erased as soon as the app stops running or moves to a new machine.

For example, let's imagine running our site using only in-memory data. When a new user signs up, we add their username to a Go map. It starts off working fine: the user can log in and add a book to their cart. But if our Go server restarts (for an update, or by accident), all the cart items and registration details will be gone. Every book review, every order, every catalog update would need to be started from scratch. If we did that, our customers wouldn't trust us, and we wouldn't be able to run a proper business or grow our user base.

The functionality of persistent storage allows us to retain:

- **`User Accounts:`** So, returning readers can sign in, see their orders or wish lists, and update info over time.
- **`Book Catalog and Inventory:`** Every title, price, stock count, and description need to be recalled instantly, even if many people browse together or the server is upgraded.
- **`Reviews, Orders, and Payments:`** Customer reviews appear immediately after posting, and orders are safely stored for record-keeping, refunds, and analytics.
- **`Site Configuration and Business Data:`** Things like sales, special banners, or admin settings should survive code deployments, so the store remains consistent for everyone.

Now, let's say a user adds a review for "Go Programming in Action." When they hit submit, our handler gets their input, writes it to the database, and (if it's successful) shows the new review to them and everyone else who visits the book's page in future. If we just relied on memory, this review would be lost as soon as the page was reloaded or the server was deployed. With persistent storage, our site becomes a living, growing history, turning a static brochure into a real destination that evolves with every customer action. In practice, the persistent storage in Go projects is almost always realised with a database, such as relational (like PostgreSQL, MySQL, or SQLite) for structured records and relationships, or sometimes NoSQL for more flexible data.

Choosing Right Database

We must know some hard truth, and that is not all databases serve the same purpose. Some excel at structured relationships and transactional safety, while others are designed for massive scalability or flexible record formats.

Relational vs. NoSQL

Relational databases like PostgreSQL, MySQL, and SQLite organize data into tables with rows and columns. They use schemas to strictly define what a user, book, or review looks like. These systems excel when our data has clear relationships, such as orders linked to users, books, and inventory counts.

For our Bookstore, relational databases let us:

- Enforce rules like "every review must belong to a book and a user"
- Easily compute totals, averages, or join information across tables (e.g., which users bought a given book)
- Support ACID transactions to guarantee data integrity even during concurrent activity
- Use SQL to write expressive queries that scale as our business grows

And, the NoSQL databases like MongoDB, Redis, and Cassandra are designed for extreme scalability, flexibility, or specialized caching. They often work best when our data is unstructured, or varies frequently. While NoSQL fits use cases like chat logs, real-time analytics, or loosely-typed storage, it doesn't usually provide the deep data integrity and reporting features needed for a professional bookstore.

How we Decide?

For catalog management, user accounts, order history, and reviews, we benefit from the familiarity and precision of relational databases. For Go, we can use PostgreSQL or MySQL with the **`database/sql`** package and supporting drivers, allowing us to define robust schemas and rely on decades of database best practices.

In some cases, we might use a NoSQL database for caching session data, recommendations, or tracking real-time events across distributed servers, but our core persistent data lives in a relational database.

Sample Program: Setting up Postgres

We will start with installing the Postgres. And, then we create databases and tables:

```
CREATE TABLE books (
    id SERIAL PRIMARY KEY,
    title VARCHAR(255) NOT NULL,
    author VARCHAR(255) NOT NULL,
    price DECIMAL(10,2) NOT NULL
);
CREATE TABLE users (
    id SERIAL PRIMARY KEY,
    username VARCHAR(64) UNIQUE NOT NULL,
    password_hash VARCHAR(255) NOT NULL
);
CREATE TABLE reviews (
    id SERIAL PRIMARY KEY,
    book_id INTEGER REFERENCES books(id),
    user_id INTEGER REFERENCES users(id),
    content TEXT NOT NULL,
    posted_at TIMESTAMP DEFAULT CURRENT_TIMESTAMP
);
```

These above schemas define every record, enforce relationships, and make querying efficient and safe. If we later want to experiment with recommendations or fast session state, we may add Redis (NoSQL) as a side component, but our main logic stays on Postgres.

Go's database/sql Package

Now, there is this called **`database/sql`** package, and it is the foundation for most of the interactions with relational databases. It provides a uniform interface for working with databases such as PostgreSQL, MySQL, and SQLite, letting us connect, run queries, insert and update records, and handle results without tying our code to any one vendor.

Connecting Database

So here, we start by importing the driver appropriate for the PostgreSQL, for example, we'd use **`github.com/lib/pq`**:

```
import (
    "database/sql"
    _ "github.com/lib/pq"
)
```

We then open a connection pool using **`sql.Open`**:

```
dsn := "host=localhost port=5432 user=postgres password=secret dbname=bookstore sslmode=disable"
db, err := sql.Open("postgres", dsn)
if err != nil {
    log.Fatal("Failed to connect to DB:", err)
}
defer db.Close()
```

This **db** object manages connections for us behind the scenes, preparing our app to handle many users at once.

Running Queries and Inserting Data

Next, let us say that we want to retrieve all books. So for this,

```
rows, err := db.Query("SELECT id, title, author, price FROM books")
if err != nil {
    log.Fatal(err)
}
defer rows.Close()
for rows.Next() {
    var id int
    var title, author string
```

```
    var price float64
    if err := rows.Scan(&id, &title, &author, &price); err !=
nil {
        log.Fatal(err)
    }
    fmt.Printf("%d: %s by %s — $%.2f\n", id, title, author,
price)
}
```

And, if we want to add a new user, we use parameterized queries to avoid SQL injection:

```
stmt := `INSERT INTO users (username, password_hash) VALUES
($1, $2) RETURNING id`
var userID int
err := db.QueryRow(stmt, "reader123",
hashedPassword).Scan(&userID)
if err != nil {
    log.Fatal(err)
}
```

Updates, Deletes, and Transactions

When we update stock after a sale, we use:

```
_, err := db.Exec("UPDATE books SET inventory=inventory-1
WHERE id=$1", bookID)
```

For more complex operations, such as placing an order (which touches orders, order_items, and updates inventory), we then wrap the steps in a transaction:

```
tx, err := db.Begin()
if err != nil { ... }
_, err = tx.Exec("UPDATE books SET inventory=inventory-1 WHERE
id=$1", bookID)
_, err = tx.Exec("INSERT INTO orders ...")
err = tx.Commit()
```

```
if err != nil {
    tx.Rollback()
    log.Fatal("Order transaction failed:", err)
}
```

Through **database/sql**, we are able to write a maintainable, portable code that works with many different databases. With our store getting busier, this package's design will try to ensure our app can scale and remain responsive. It shall be reliably handling every book and user stored in our system.

Robust Transactions and Business Logic

We're not just talking basic CRUD here, we're diving into transactional operations and making sure your data is consistent. These are the areas where persistent storage really shines in professional applications. When our Bookstore needs to process an order, a bunch of database actions happen at once: we decrease inventory, save the order record, and potentially update user history. We bundle these actions together in a transaction so they all succeed or fail as one unit.

In Go, we initiate a transaction using **db.Begin()**. Every SQL action, like updating inventory or inserting the order, uses the **tx** transaction object. Only when all steps succeed do we call **tx.Commit()**; otherwise, any error triggers a **tx.Rollback()**, ensuring no partial data changes make it into the database.

Following is an order workflow:

```
tx, err := db.Begin()
if err != nil { return err }
_, err = tx.Exec("UPDATE books SET inventory=inventory-1 WHERE id=$1 AND inventory>0", bookID)
if err != nil {
    tx.Rollback()
    return err
}
_, err = tx.Exec("INSERT INTO orders (user_id, book_id, created_at) VALUES ($1, $2, now())", userID, bookID)
if err != nil {
    tx.Rollback()
```

```
    return err
}
return tx.Commit()
```

This above pattern is quite a vital for checkout, refunds, user deletions, or batch catalog updates. If deleting a user, we place all associated SQL deletes inside a transaction, ensuring removal happens only if all related data (reviews, orders) are properly cleared. It also keeps our analytics data correct, ensuring sales reflect only completed orders and inventory always matches actual on-hand books.

To go beyond simple CRUD, we focus on transactional operations and data consistency, areas where persistent storage shines in professional applications. When our Bookstore needs to process an order, several database actions must occur together: decreasing inventory, saving the order record, and potentially updating user history. We wrap these actions in a transaction so they all succeed or fail as one unit.

Strengthening Security

Enforcing Constraints

Sometimes, we will not find it enough to simply store data. We will be in need of a guarantee that every piece of information is valid, connected, and secure. So here, the first line of defense is enforcing constraints at the database level. We use primary keys to ensure every record is unique, foreign keys to associate reviews and orders with real users and books, and checks to limit values (for example, rating between 1 and 5).

In our schema, the constraint will look like this:

```
CREATE TABLE reviews (
    id SERIAL PRIMARY KEY,
    book_id INTEGER REFERENCES books(id),
    user_id INTEGER REFERENCES users(id),
    rating INTEGER CHECK (rating BETWEEN 1 AND 5),
    comment TEXT
);
```

Now here, no review can exist without a real book or user, and every rating is within an expected range.

Preventing SQL Injection

Let us quickly get into the security aspect and it should be also a top priority. Here, we store sensitive information like passwords only as strong hashes, never plain text. So here, we use libraries like **bcrypt**:

```
import "golang.org/x/crypto/bcrypt"
hash, err := bcrypt.GenerateFromPassword([]byte(password),
bcrypt.DefaultCost)
```

When authenticating, we compare the hash to the user's input, never directly storing or retrieving actual passwords. For every query, we will use the parameterization to guard against SQL injection attacks. And, instead of building queries using string concatenation, we will pass the user input as separate parameters:

```
stmt := `SELECT id FROM users WHERE username=$1`
err := db.QueryRow(stmt, username).Scan(&id)
```

This will ensure us that the malicious input can't rewrite queries or access unauthorized data.

Together, constraints, transactions, password hashing, safe queries, and validation form a robust, secure data layer for our Bookstore. These practices prevent lost orders, orphaned reviews, or security breaches, and build lasting trust with every customer who visits our site. With integrity and security in place, we're well-prepared to explore ORMs, optimize with indexes, and scale confidently.

ORMs for Rapid Development

A lot of bookstore apps start with raw SQL to make things clearer, but as our data models and relationships grow, we might want faster feature development and easier maintenance. This is where ORMs, or Object-Relational Mappers, come in, they let us define Go structs that directly map to database tables, automate migrations, easily manage associations, and perform common operations with less boilerplate.

GORM is a popular ORM for Go. With GORM, we just declare our models as shown below:

```
type Book struct {
    gorm.Model
    Title   string
    Author  string
```

```
    Price   float64
    Reviews []Review
}
type Review struct {
    gorm.Model
    BookID  uint
    UserID  uint
    Rating  int
    Comment string
}
```

The GORM makes use of struct tags and conventions to auto-create foreign keys and relationships. Using them, we can migrate the schemas automatically as below:

```
db.AutoMigrate(&Book{}, &Review{})
```

After this, we then create a new book or adding a review is now a single concise call, without hand-writing an INSERT:

```
book := Book{Title: "Pro Go", Author: "Smith", Price: 29.99}
db.Create(&book)
review := Review{BookID: book.ID, UserID: 1, Rating: 5,
Comment: "Great read!"}
db.Create(&review)
```

And, the fetching of books with their reviews is also easy:

```
var books []Book
db.Preload("Reviews").Find(&books)
```

Although ORMs like GORM make rapid development easy and keep the code clean, they should be used thoughtfully – for example, by switching to raw SQL for high-performance reporting or unusual queries when needed.

When we use an ORM, it speeds up how quickly we can launch features, keeps our code safe from common SQL mistakes, and updates our Bookstore's data models with minimal fuss as business requirements change.

Optimizing Performance

Indexes are basically like indexes in a book, helping us find the info we need super quickly. If you put indexes on the columns you search, sort or join on most often, you'll make queries faster and keep your app snappy.

Types of Indexes

The most basic index is on primary keys, which every table gets by default. Searching by **`id`** is always quick. But for real-world queries, such as filtering books by author, price, or title, or finding all reviews for a book, we add indexes to those fields:

```
CREATE INDEX idx_books_author ON books(author);
CREATE INDEX idx_books_title_price ON books(title, price);
CREATE INDEX idx_reviews_book_id ON reviews(book_id);
```

The composite indexes (multiple columns) help with common multi-field searches, like "find all books by a certain author under $20."

The partial indexes target only a subset of rows, for example, "books in stock":

```
CREATE INDEX idx_books_in_stock ON books(inventory) WHERE
inventory > 0;
```

With proper indexing, finding the top 10 best-selling titles or all reviews for a given book takes milliseconds, not seconds. This pleasant, responsive experience is what keeps users coming back and ensures our backend can handle larger visitor counts.

Apart from the optimized indexes, we can also use the advanced SQL to extract rich insights. These queries let us answer important questions, power user dashboards, and guide business decisions, which are going far beyond simple lookups.

Joins to Combine Data

For example, to see every review and its author for a given book, we can do:

```
SELECT reviews.comment, reviews.rating, users.username
FROM reviews
JOIN users ON reviews.user_id = users.id
WHERE reviews.book_id = 42;
```

This present review summaries directly on the product pages and enables deeper analysis, such as highlighting top contributors.

Aggregations for Summaries and Trends

To find our best-selling books, we aggregate sales data:

```
SELECT books.title, COUNT(orders.id) AS sales_count
FROM books
JOIN orders ON books.id = orders.book_id
GROUP BY books.title
ORDER BY sales_count DESC
LIMIT 10;
```

These queries underpin bestseller lists, inform reordering decisions, and drive promotional campaigns.

Subqueries and Complex Filtering

Suppose we want books reviewed by users who have placed more than five orders:

```
SELECT title FROM books
WHERE id IN (
    SELECT book_id FROM reviews
    WHERE user_id IN (
        SELECT user_id FROM orders
        GROUP BY user_id HAVING COUNT(*) > 5
    )
);
```

The subqueries let us analyze deep user engagement, target loyal readers, or personalize recommendations.

For admin reporting or dashboards, we can build queries using joins, groups, and computed fields, like average review ratings, weekly sales totals, or identifying users with abandoned carts. Every advanced query supports features users expect in a modern Bookstore, such as "recommended for you," "top authors this month," or "your recent purchases."

Summary

So, we figured out how important it is to have persistent storage in web apps by looking at how databases make things durable, reliable and personalised for the Bookstore's features. We looked at how choosing the right database and designing the schema well can support user accounts, inventories, reviews and transactional records, both in day-to-day operations and in future scalability. We were able to connect, query and modify records efficiently thanks to hands-on development with Go's database/SQL package, and real-world examples showed us how transactions guarantee data consistency and prevent errors during multi-step operations like checkouts or batch updates.

We also made things more secure and reliable by using constraints, validation, hashed passwords and parameterised queries, which built trust by protecting customer data and application health. We sped up development and made managing models easier by using ORMs like GORM, but we still kept direct access to SQL for important performance tasks. We used strategic indexing and connection management to speed up query response times and get the Bookstore ready for more users and bigger datasets. We used advanced SQL queries to generate analytic insights, useful reports and personalised recommendations, turning raw data into something we could act on and into something that would engage users.

Chapter 6: Concurrency in Go

We've been working on Go web development, and it's shown how important it is to build apps that are robust, maintainable and efficient. So far, we've been busy getting the foundations of our Bookstore project in place, working on things like routing, handlers, data management and scalability. The more our app grows, the more important it is going to be to make sure it can handle thousands of users at the same time. It's all about being able to do more with less, you know, like serving super-fast pages, handling lots of requests at once and delivering real-time features, without losing any data integrity or performance.

So, in this chapter, we're going to take a look at how concurrency works, and the principles behind it. We'll work together to find the tools and patterns that'll help our Bookstore thrive in the tough world of modern web apps. In this day and age, you can't just hope to be fast and responsive, you have to be. It's not just a technical feature, it's a way of thinking that guides how we design, set up and run our systems, making sure everyone who uses them has a great experience.

Age of Rapid Applications

In today's digital landscape, user patience is at an all-time low and expectations for instantaneous results are at an all-time high. Even a delay of a few hundred milliseconds can lead to a measurable reduction in user engagement, loyalty, and ultimately, profitability. Fast, highly-responsive web applications are not just desirable, they are essential for staying competitive. Every fraction of a second counts: slow page loads, laggy search results, and delayed transactions all contribute to user dissatisfaction and abandonment.

User Experience and Business Impact

How responsive a platform is affects how users perceive both the platform and the brand. It's all about trust and reputation in our Bookstore app, so every interaction, whether it's searching for a title or completing a purchase, is super important for long-term success. With so many options just a click away, users expect instant feedback. If you can do that, you'll get more loyal customers, better conversion rates and a competitive edge.

Factors like application speed, network infrastructure, server hardware and database performance all have an impact, but at the end of the day, how the software is designed is really important. The way things are normally done, where tasks are done one after the other, makes things less responsive because each user has to wait their turn, which increases latency as the system gets bigger.

The trick to getting around sequential bottlenecks is concurrency, which is basically the ability to juggle multiple tasks at the same time rather than waiting in line. So for our bookstore, it's all about handling book searches, user authentication, and purchase processing at the same time. This makes sure that users get fast results, even when there's a lot of traffic.

Go's Concurrency Philosophy

The concept of concurrency for Go is a foundational principle, not an afterthought. Its goroutines are lightweight and efficient, providing the backbone for responsive server-side logic that can scale to thousands of simultaneous users with modest hardware overhead file:2. Combined with channels for safe data exchange, Go's model enables efficient coordination and management of complex, data-intensive workloads, precisely the environment required for modern web applications.

And this concurrency can be used in various ways like:

- Book search requests can be fulfilled in parallel, with each genre or filter handled by a goroutine and results merged for instant browsing.
- User interactions, such as posting reviews or updating carts, remain swift and independent, unfettered by busy server routines.
- The bookstore can process bulk operations, for example, flash sales or promotional events, accommodating thousands of buyers in real time without sacrificing reliability.

The most sophisticated and highly-responsive applications are no longer a luxury but a mandate for user satisfaction and business growth. The Go's concurrency model brings the capability to meet these demands confidently and efficiently. As we delve deeper into this chapter, we will apply these foundational concepts toward practical performance improvements, evolving both our project and our understanding of modern software engineering.

Principles of Concurrency

We might come across tasks that naturally overlap, like serving search requests, processing orders, updating inventory and handling reviews, all for lots of users at the same time. If we reply to each user one at a time, it'll slow down the experience and might even overwhelm the system during busy times. This is a common problem with modern web services, where users expect instant feedback and constant interaction.

GO was designed by Google developers to tackle these problems head-on, offering concurrency as a built-in solution rather than an afterthought. The language makes it a breeze to model these overlapping activities, combining simplicity with performance and scalability.

What Is Concurrency?

Concurrency is all about making a program so that lots of tasks can run at the same time, instead of each one waiting for the other to finish. In Go, this means we can handle new search queries, process checkouts and update reviews all at the same time, making sure no one is held up by someone else's activity. To the user, our bookstore feels snappy and always available, even when hundreds interact at once.

I'll give you an example: think of a team of librarians working together. One is on the phone answering book enquiries, another is keeping an eye on the stock, and a third is getting the orders out. Each librarian works on their own, but they make sure that customers always get help quickly. In Go, each concurrent task is managed by its own independent routines, with a lightweight "scheduler" overseeing things to make sure everything runs smoothly and in coordination.

Goroutines in Action

The Go's concurrency leverages goroutines, lightweight functions managed by the Go runtime. Starting a goroutine is as simple as prefixing a function call with **go**. Each goroutine functions independently, yet shares memory with others, enabling powerful patterns, but also requiring disciplined management to avoid conflicts.

Let us think of a situation that we want our bookstore's backend to search books and check their stock in parallel:

```
package main
import (
    "fmt"
    "time"
)
// Simulate book search
func searchBooks(query string) {
    time.Sleep(1 * time.Second)
    fmt.Println("Books found for query:", query)
}
// Simulate inventory check
func checkInventory(bookID int) {
    time.Sleep(2 * time.Second)
    fmt.Println("Inventory checked for book:", bookID)
}
func main() {
    go searchBooks("Concurrency in Go")
    go checkInventory(101)
    fmt.Println("Bookstore is serving requests...")
```

```
    time.Sleep(3 * time.Second) // Let goroutines finish
}
```

When we run this, both operations proceed side by side, and our application remains responsive. The program can initiate more goroutines for other tasks, scaling gracefully as requests flood in.

Sample Program: Scaling Bookstore

Now, what if we want to handle a bunch of user reviews at the same time, and write each one straight to the database as soon as we get it?

```
func processReview(userID int, review string) {
    // Simulate writing to database
    time.Sleep(1 * time.Second)
    fmt.Printf("Processed review from user %d: %s\n", userID,
review)
}
func main() {
    reviews := []struct{ userID int; text string }{
        {101, "Great Go book!"},
        {102, "Loved the examples."},
        {103, "Fast checkout experience."},
    }
    for _, r := range reviews {
        go processReview(r.userID, r.text)
    }
    time.Sleep(2 * time.Second)
    fmt.Println("All reviews processed concurrently.")
}
```

From the above code, the bookstore can swiftly process multiple actions together, ensuring high throughput and happy customers, even during busy periods.

If you want to do more with it, you could try launching some goroutines for extra tasks, like checking stock, sending notifications or updating recommendations. You can see how quickly you can handle requests, and experiment with more users and tasks.

Serving Concurrent Requests using Goroutines

Traditional threads are expensive, but goroutines are cheap and you can spawn thousands of them, so Go applications can efficiently handle lots of actions at the same time. The Go runtime handles scheduling, so developers can focus on the logic without getting bogged down in the complexities of manual thread management.

To clarify, let's think about a scenario where the Bookstore gets book search requests, review submissions and purchase actions all at once. A sequential server would handle these one by one, causing delays as users wait in line. With goroutines, each action works independently, so whether 10 or 10,000 users are online, everyone gets a pretty instant response.

In the following sample program, the Bookstore is looking to process several book searches at once, perhaps users are filtering by different genres. So here, we assign each search to a goroutine and collect results as soon as they finish:

```
package main
import (
    "fmt"
    "time"
)
type Book struct {
    Title string
    Genre string
}
// Simulate database search by genre
func searchBooksByGenre(genre string, ch chan<- []Book) {
    time.Sleep(1 * time.Second)
    books := []Book{{Title: "Concurrency in Go", Genre:
genre}}
    ch <- books
}
func main() {
    genres := []string{"Sci-Fi", "Fantasy", "Mystery"}
    resultsChannel := make(chan []Book, len(genres))
```

```
    for _, genre := range genres {
        go searchBooksByGenre(genre, resultsChannel)
    }
    var allBooks []Book
    for i := 0; i < len(genres); i++ {
        books := <-resultsChannel
        allBooks = append(allBooks, books...)
    }
    fmt.Println("All search results:", allBooks)
}
```

Each genre search is performed by a separate goroutine. The result channels aggregate the output, allowing the user interface to remain fast and responsive, even with many simultaneous requests.

This allow our Bookstore to process reviews, fulfill orders, send notifications, and update recommendations simultaneously, ensuring every user's interaction is swift and uninterrupted. A large sale or seasonal spike won't slow us down, each event can be distributed among dozens or hundreds of goroutines, scaling effortlessly as our reader community grows.

Goroutines Channeling

We've found that concurrency is great for web apps like our Bookstore, but if there's no way for goroutines to talk to each other, it can lead to problems. Go has these channels that are designed to sync up and safely transfer data between goroutines. Imagine channels as special pipelines where only messages that are complete get through. Every message is sent and received, so no information is missed and no task can move forward without the data it needs.

Think about a team of librarians updating a catalogue and checking out books for customers. Instead of shouting across the room, each librarian sends written notes through a pneumatic tube system. These tubes (channels) make sure everything is delivered in the right order and that nobody can mess up. They make sure that each message is dealt with one at a time, which keeps the catalogue accurate and makes sure the transactions are safe.

Building Channels

The channels are straightforward to create and use, and are central to safe concurrency. The simplest channel transmits a value of a specific type:

```go
bookChannel := make(chan string) // Channel for book titles
```

- Sending data:

```go
bookChannel <- "Concurrency in Go"
```

- Receiving data:

```go
title := <-bookChannel
```

The channels can also be set up for single-direction use (only send or only receive), which improves safety and guarantees that goroutines play their intended roles, ideal for structured workflows like order processing or billing in Bookstore.

Sample Program: Parallel Book Search & Aggregated Results

In the following sample program, we'll check out how the Bookstore can search multiple genres at once and combine the results, sending data across different processes for structured completion.

```go
package main

import (
    "fmt"
    "time"
)

type Book struct {
    Title string
    Genre string
}

// Search a genre and send results on channel
func searchBooksByGenre(genre string, ch chan<- []Book) {
    time.Sleep(1 * time.Second)
    books := []Book{{Title: "Concurrency in Go", Genre:
genre}}
    ch <- books // Channeling result safely
}
```

```
func main() {
    genres := []string{"Sci-Fi", "Fantasy", "Mystery"}
    results := make(chan []Book, len(genres)) // Buffered for parallel goroutines
    for _, genre := range genres {
        go searchBooksByGenre(genre, results)
    }
    var allBooks []Book
    for i := 0; i < len(genres); i++ {
        books := <-results // Receiving each processed result
        allBooks = append(allBooks, books...)
    }
    fmt.Println("Aggregated search results:", allBooks)
}
```

From the above program, we can observe that the buffered channels (**make(chan []Book, len(genres))**) allow goroutines to finish without blocking on immediate receives, crucial for scaling parallel searches. And, the channel send/receive operations keep the workflow synchronized, no update is lost or duplicated, no result arrives before processing is complete.

Channel Directions and Multiplexing

In this program, we can also specify the channels for send-only or receive-only activity, incase we want to reduce the error risk for collaborative goroutines:

```
func processOrder(ch chan<- Order) { /* send only */ }
func billOrder(ch <-chan Order) { /* receive only */ }
```

And, for more sophisticated workflows, such as waiting on review completions and feedback simultaneously, We can use the **select** to listen on multiple channels at once:

```
select {
case order := <-ordersChannel:
    processOrder(order)
case feedback := <-feedbackChannel:
```

```
    handleFeedback(feedback)
default:
    fmt.Println("Waiting for updates...")
}
```

In the above script, the **select** block ensures the Bookstore backend remains responsive even as different tasks compete for server attention, no goroutine blocks unnecessarily, and all results are processed as soon as they're ready.

Buffered Channels and Graceful Shutdown

The buffered channels are especially useful when batching operations like reviews, orders, or notifications. They allow sending goroutines to complete work independently of receiver readiness, useful in high-traffic scenarios. After all processing, channels should be closed for predictable shutdown and resource cleaning:

```
close(bookChannel)
// Use range to iterate remaining buffered data
for title := range bookChannel {
    fmt.Println("Processed title:", title)
}
```

Now while we make use of the channels, following key things we must keep in mind:

- The first is that we must share data only through channels for thread safety.
- We must focus on IO-bound or blocking operations for real concurrency gains.
- We must simulate both heavy load and error scenarios, and for this we can use Go's testing package to benchmark and catch concurrency bugs early.
- And, the last is that we must limit the channel buffer sizes to optimize memory and avoid overflows.

When you get channeling down, it takes our Bookstore app from basic concurrency to a more sophisticated, orchestrated communication system. And that makes it super responsive, reliable and scalable for every reader, whatever the workload.

Up and Running with Synchronization

Race Condition

The biggest risk of concurrency is the race condition, which is when two or more goroutines access shared state without coordination, and at least one is a write. The results of a race are always unpredictable, and the bugs that are created are really hard to reproduce and fix. For the bookstore, this could mean inventory counts that go up and down for no reason, orders that get put in the wrong place, or user data that gets corrupted when updates are happening at the same time.

For example, imagine two users checking out the last copy of "Concurrency in Go" at the same time. If both of these happen at the same time, the final count could be negative, or even worse, the sale could be double-booked. It's really important to protect all shared resources, like databases, maps, slices and values representing current stock, whenever there's a chance more than one person will access them at the same time.

Synchronization Primitives

The Go provides several robust primitives to prevent race conditions and ensure coordinated operation:

- **sync.WaitGroup** aggregates parallel operations and blocks until all are finished, vital for workflows that depend on complete processing before advancing, such as batch search aggregation or multi-step purchases.
- **sync.Mutex** provides mutual exclusion, locking access to critical sections so only one goroutine can alter shared data at a time. Mutexes are indispensable for inventory updates, user data changes, or any mutable state shared across goroutines.

WaitGroup

A WaitGroup acts like a team leader's checklist: each goroutine checks in (with **`Add`**), signals completion (**`Done`**), and the main process waits (**`Wait`**) until everyone's finished. This avoids partial results and guarantees consistent states before output.

Mutex

A Mutex is essentially a traffic light: only one concurrent worker (goroutine) can enter the protected area for a period, performs the update, and then releases the lock for the next. Proper locking prevents overlapping writes and ensures correctness even under high traffic.

Combining Orchestration and Protection

The sophisticated workflows often require both WaitGroups for orchestrating work and Mutexes for guarding critical sections. For instance, let us take a sample program of processing bulk orders which means many goroutines may need to update inventory. But here, only by wrapping those updates inside **`mutex.Lock()`** / **`mutex.Unlock()`**, the Bookstore can guarantee that every sale and stock update happens accurately and without conflict.

Following is the sample script:

```
var wg sync.WaitGroup
var mutex sync.Mutex
func processOrder(order Order) {
    defer wg.Done()
    for _, item := range order.Items {
        mutex.Lock() // One goroutine at a time per inventory
update
        inventory[item.BookName] -= item.Quantity
        mutex.Unlock()
    }
}
// Launch several concurrent order processors
for _, order := range bulkOrders {
    wg.Add(1)
    go processOrder(order)
}
wg.Wait() // Only proceed once all updates are complete
```

When you chain these mechanisms together, the app gets the benefits of concurrency without losing data integrity or risking silent errors. And if you can get synchronisation right, you're on the road to creating web apps that are not only fast but also reliable, correct and easy to expand into new areas. It makes sure the Bookstore can handle any number of customers at the same time without ever putting their experience or your business's integrity at risk.

Implement Concurrent Cache

A cache speeds up web services by storing frequently-accessed data in memory, dramatically reducing database loads and response times. In a concurrent environment, where many users may read from and write to the cache at the same time, ensuring safety is paramount. An unsynchronized cache risks corrupting data or crashing the app. Our Bookstore needs not only a fast but a reliably managed cache system, resilient under thousands of simultaneous requests.

Cache Structure and Data Safety

A concurrent cache typically combines a map (for fast key-value lookups) with a **sync.Mutex** to protect the store during updates. Without locking, parallel writes or deletions could interleave and leave the cache in an unpredictable state.

A good cache should support:

- Safe simultaneous reading and writing from multiple goroutines
- Efficient eviction (removing stale entries when the cache is full)
- Fast access for both hot and cold data

Implementing Book Details Cache

The given below is a sample program for a thread-safe cache for storing book details.

```
type BookDetails struct {
    Title  string
    Author string
    Price  float64
}
type ConcurrentCache struct {
    data  map[string]BookDetails
    mutex sync.Mutex
}
// Store adds a book to the cache, locking for safety
func (c *ConcurrentCache) Store(key string, value BookDetails)
{
    c.mutex.Lock()
    c.data[key] = value
    c.mutex.Unlock()
}
// Fetch retrieves from cache, locking to prevent race
conditions
func (c *ConcurrentCache) Fetch(key string) (BookDetails,
bool) {
    c.mutex.Lock()
```

```
    value, exists := c.data[key]
    c.mutex.Unlock()
    return value, exists
}
func main() {
    cache := &ConcurrentCache{
        data: make(map[string]BookDetails),
    }
    // Simulate concurrent storage
    var wg sync.WaitGroup
    for i := 0; i < 5; i++ {
        wg.Add(1)
        go func(id int) {
            defer wg.Done()
            book := BookDetails{Title: fmt.Sprintf("Book %d",
id), Author: "Author", Price: 99.99}
            cache.Store(fmt.Sprintf("ID%d", id), book)
        }(i)
    }
    wg.Wait()
    // Simulate concurrent fetches
    for i := 0; i < 5; i++ {
        wg.Add(1)
        go func(id int) {
            defer wg.Done()
            if details, ok := cache.Fetch(fmt.Sprintf("ID%d",
id)); ok {
                fmt.Printf("Fetched from cache: %+v\n",
details)
            }
```

```
        }(i)
    }
    wg.Wait()
}
```

From the above program,

- The locking on both **Store** and **Fetch** is able to keep every read and write atomic. With this, no two goroutines ever corrupt the internal map.
- And, the use of **sync.WaitGroup** has llowed us to launch multiple concurrent cache operations, which is crucial for high-volume web workloads.

Eviction and Resource Limits

To prevent runaway memory usage, caches need an eviction policy. While full-featured LRU strategies exist, the given below is a simple size-based eviction handled safely in a concurrent context:

```
const MAXCACHESIZE = 1000
func (c *ConcurrentCache) CheckEviction() {
    c.mutex.Lock()
    if len(c.data) > MAXCACHESIZE {
        // Remove an arbitrary key (for demo, first one found)
        for key := range c.data {
            delete(c.data, key)
            break
        }
    }
    c.mutex.Unlock()
}
```

In the above, we can call **CheckEviction** after each write to protect against uncontrolled growth.

If we expand this example, we can handle reviews, recommendations and images too. We can introduce eviction and simulate hundreds of parallel requests. We can also measure how quickly things load when there's a lot of traffic, and see how the Bookstore can handle it all without any problems. Basically, by building a strong cache that works in the background, our Bookstore becomes fast and resilient, ready for whatever the real world throws at it and lots of users, with every cache operation managed safely in a modern Go style.

Summary

So, we got a good idea of how concurrency improves the design of Go web applications. We looked at why highly responsive systems are important, how goroutines allow for simple parallel operations, and how channels make it safe and easy to communicate between routines running at the same time. In the Bookstore project, we used synchronization primitives like WaitGroup and Mutex to make sure data integrity was kept, avoiding race conditions during high-volume sales and batch updates. We also put in place a thread-safe cache to protect shared state and control eviction to keep performance high even under load. We did stress tests and tweaked our locking strategies, and that showed us how strong, flexible, and accurate systems can be if you put a bit of thought into concurrency design. And that means we are all set to build Go services that can handle massive amounts of real-world traffic without losing any accuracy or performance.

CHAPTER 7: SESSIONS, AUTHENTICATION, AND AUTHORIZATION

Now that our Bookstore app is getting bigger and supporting more features and users than ever before, it's really important to have strong identity, state, and security. Having a responsive design and fast backends isn't enough if users can't enjoy personalised experiences, manage purchases safely, or trust the platform with their information. This chapter will tell you everything you need to know about user sessions, secure authentication and authorisation systems – the true backbone of modern web applications built with Go.

We'll take a look at the architecture that makes every visitor a recognised user, their session lasting even if the page is reloaded or if lots of people are logged in at once. We'll also take a look at how web session management has evolved, the building blocks of cookies and tokens, and the modern techniques for protecting passwords, data, and sensitive operations. It doesn't matter if our users sign in with Bookstore credentials or via integrated OAuth/Social providers, their trust and security are never compromised. All the technical explorations are part of the ongoing Bookstore project, using real code, thoughtful commentary and progressive complexity to make sure all the new and existing features fit together seamlessly.

Principles of User Session Management

All the pages, preferences and actions for each user are tied together by something called 'Sessions'. In the Bookstore, sessions save your cart, show you personalised book recommendations and keep your identity without you having to log in again and again. As web browsers operate over the stateless HTTP protocol, all context is lost between requests unless we intentionally bridge the gap. This is where sessions come in. They create temporary storage, either in the browser, on the backend, or via distributed systems, tying actions and data to each user, sometimes for minutes, sometimes for weeks.

If there aren't sessions, navigating from search results to checkout would mean losing content, wiping preferences and breaking the rhythm of user engagement. Now, what if there was a reader who really looked into rare titles, put them in their cart, and then got interrupted? But, hey, no worries, sessions make sure nothing's lost, and they can just pick up right where they left off. Even simple things, like greeting a returning user by name, rely on session continuity. But actually, sessions are more than just a bonus. They're essential for privacy, trust, and security. They carry authentication details, permission info and sensitive preferences, so they need to be managed carefully and regularly audited.

Storage Strategies

The web applications can manage session data in several ways, each with clear trade-offs:

- Client-Side Storage

The best thing about storing session tokens or fragments in secure cookies is that it's lightweight and won't strain backend resources. But there are strict limits on what you can do with the browser, and security risks like XSS and CSRF, so it's best to use it only for basic stuff and never to store sensitive data without encrypting it. For example, session tokens should always be signed and set with Secure/HTTPOnly flags, and time-limited to stop abuse.

- Server-Side Storage

A lot of bookstore session records are stored in backend memory, files or external caches (like Redis). Memory-based stores are fast but short-lived, and sessions disappear if servers restart, which can frustrate users. It's true that file-based storage is still around, but it can degrade if a lot of people use it at the same time, unless you've got the right indexing in place. We use Redis or SQL databases to handle millions of active sessions, with rapid access and clear expiry workflows. It's all about finding the right balance between speed, reliability and security when it comes to choosing a storage backend.

- Hybrid and Distributed Architectures

As our Bookstore outgrows single-server hosting, it benefits from distributed session management, ensuring continuity even as users jump across different backend nodes. This strategy demands unique session IDs, portable tokens, and centralized audit trails, all designed for seamless failover and scale.

Sample Program: Go Session Management

Following is a minimal illustration, using secure cookie sessions:

```
import (
    "net/http"
    "time"
)
func setSession(w http.ResponseWriter, token string) {
    http.SetCookie(w, &http.Cookie{
        Name:     "session_token",
        Value:    token,
        Expires:  time.Now().Add(2 * time.Hour),
        HttpOnly: true,
        Secure:   true,
        SameSite: http.SameSiteStrictMode,
    })
}
```

```
func getSession(r *http.Request) (string, error) {
    cookie, err := r.Cookie("session_token")
    if err != nil {
        return "", err
    }
    return cookie.Value, nil
}
```

Now here, me must ensure that we always apply Secure, HTTPOnly, and SameSite flags. The sessions should expire meaningfully, no perpetual tokens.

Scalable Session Storage Strategies

The more people who use Bookstore, the more important it becomes to manage sessions. It's a lot to handle, with thousands of sessions happening at once. You've got to be smart about where and how you store session data, and make sure it's fast, reliable, and secure.

Client-Side Storage

Client-side session storage relies on cookies or browser mechanisms. It minimizes backend complexity since each user carries their context, but browsers strictly limit storage. For Bookstore, cookies proved handy for small data, session tokens, limited preferences, user identifiers, but never secure credentials or rich cart data. Cookies must always be flagged as HTTPOnly, Secure, SameSite, and carefully encrypted if holding even modestly sensitive details. Mismanagement here exposes users to XSS and CSRF attacks, risking identity theft or unauthorized actions.

Following is a simple demonstration of the Cookie Session Setup:

```
http.SetCookie(w, &http.Cookie{
    Name:     "session_token",
    Value:    token,
    Expires:  time.Now().Add(2 * time.Hour),
    HttpOnly: true,
    Secure:   true,
    SameSite: http.SameSiteStrictMode,
```

```
})
```

Here, each flag bolsters protection against common web threats. The expiry ensures sessions are time-bound and not perpetual.

Server-Side Storage

Most modern web sessions reside on the backend, either in-memory, files, or external stores. Memory-based sessions are fast but vanish on server restart, an annoyance during Bookstore upgrades. File-based approaches offer durability but slow down with heavy traffic unless indexed. For scaling across many servers, distributed session stores (like Redis, Memcached, or SQL databases) are essential, they provide rapid access, automatic expiration, and resilience against node failures.

Following is the example of Redis Integration to understand it better:

```
store, _ := redistore.NewRediStore(10, "tcp",
"localhost:6379", "", []byte("secret-key"))
session, _ := store.Get(r, "session-name")
session.Values["userid"] = 12345
session.Save(r, w)
```

Here, with the use of Redis, sessions persisted even as Bookstore scaled horizontally, avoiding dropped carts and lost logins during traffic surges.

Distributed and Hybrid Models

We've seen Bookstore grow and grow, and it's withstood server restarts, traffic spikes and code deployments. With everything stored in one place and each session having its own ID, it was easy to move between the different parts of the system, which is exactly what you need when you're dealing with millions of requests a day. They're a combo of memory caching for speed and persistent database layers for reliability. All the carts and user IDs were kept in Redis, while the deep history and preferences were stored in SQL, mapped by session tokens.

Each session strategy included regular audits, strong encryption, HTTPS-only transmission, and instant purge on logout or expiry. We did routine reviews to make sure that session stores didn't leak, and secrets used for signing tokens were rotated on schedule. We made sure to renew tokens regularly and to set strong session expiration practices, which kept any stale data from causing any problems.

Secure Cookie Handling

We all know that cookies are key to managing sessions and states in web apps, but they're also a major target for attackers because they handle sensitive stuff like session tokens, user identifiers and preferences. If the bookstore handles cookies wrong, it could lead to people stealing your details, making unauthorised purchases or invading your privacy. This is because as the user base grows and the stakes rise, cookie security becomes more and more important.

The attackers exploit cookies via two main vectors:

- Cross-Site Scripting (**XSS**) in which the malicious scripts steal cookies from the browser, accessing session tokens and impersonating users. And,
- Cross-Site Request Forgery (**CSRF**) in which attackers trick browsers into sending authenticated requests, leveraging active cookies to perform unwanted actions.

And, therefore, all cookies in the Bookstore carrying any authentication or state must be protected with robust attributes and, where possible, encryption.

The Four Pillars

HTTPOnly Attribute

This makes cookies invisible to client-side JavaScript, drastically reducing the attack surface for XSS. In Go:

```
http.SetCookie(w, &http.Cookie{
    Name:     "session_token",
    Value:    token,
    HttpOnly: true,
})
```

If **`HttpOnly`** is set, even after an XSS breach, the cookies are inaccessible to scripts.

Secure Attribute

This only sends cookies over HTTPS connections, blocking interception over unsecured networks.

```
http.SetCookie(w, &http.Cookie{
    Name:   "session_token",
    Value:  token,
    Secure: true,
})
```

Just make sure you always use HTTPS and never accept insecure connections for session-related operations.

SameSite Attribute

This prevents cookies from being sent with cross-site requests, defeating most CSRF attacks.

```
http.SetCookie(w, &http.Cookie{
    Name:     "session_token",
    Value:    token,
    SameSite: http.SameSiteStrictMode,
})
```

We use the **StrictMode** for session cookies, only allow transmission for direct navigation within your app.

Expiration and Prudent Lifespan

The expiry date on sensitive cookies should always be short. If cookies live for a long time, there's a risk of session hijack, so it's really important to immediately expire them when you log out.

```
http.SetCookie(w, &http.Cookie{
    Name:    "session_token",
    Value:   token,
    Expires: time.Now().Add(2 * time.Hour),
})
```

And, we must not use perpetual or "remember me" cookies for core authentication without explicit user consent and enhanced security.

Cookie Values Encryption

The plain session tokens are vulnerable even with properly set attributes. If we encrypt cookie values, then it ensures that, if intercepted, no meaningful information is exposed. And, here we use **crypto/aes**, **crypto/cipher** to encrypt data before it is placed in a cookie.

Following is a quick example on the encryption of a cookie value:

```
import (
    "crypto/aes"
```

```
    "crypto/cipher"
)
func encryptCookieValue(plainText string, key []byte) (string,
error) {
    block, err := aes.NewCipher(key)
    // ... encryption logic, return ciphertext as string
}
```

We then wrap the encrypted values with strong error handling.

Implement User Authentication

The way we do this is by making sure that the Bookstore users can be sure that they're who they say they are. It lets you have persistent accounts, protected shopping carts, private reviews and more, while stopping impersonation and unauthorised access. These web applications need to have login workflows that are solid, simple for users, and able to withstand modern attacks.

Authentication Flow

The typical flows include registration (storing credentials securely), login (validating credentials), session preservation (so users stay signed in across requests), and logout (cleanly ending access). At registration, the Bookstore never stores plain-text passwords. It uses bcrypt to hash each password, transforming it into a secure string that cannot be reversed. When users log in, their password is hashed and compared to the stored hash. If matched, the user is recognized, and the system creates a session token.

Let us take an example of a user model and password storage:

```
type User struct {
    ID       int
    Username string
    Password string // Store only hashed password
}
```

In the above, the Storage in the database only includes the bcrypt-hashed password.

Validating User Credentials

Next, when a user attempts login, the server retrieves the stored hash and compares it to the hash of the entered password.

```
func LoginUser(username, enteredPassword string) bool {
    storedHashedPassword := retrieveHash(username)
    err := bcrypt.CompareHashAndPassword(storedHashedPassword,
[]byte(enteredPassword))
    return err == nil
}
```

The successful logins yield a fresh session token. They are flagged with HTTPOnly and Secure attributes in the user's browser cookie.

Maintaining Authentication State

Once authenticated, the Bookstore needs to preserve login state between requests. This is achieved by setting a signed session cookie:

```
http.SetCookie(w, &http.Cookie{
    Name:     "session_token",
    Value:    generatedToken,
    HttpOnly: true,
    Secure:   true,
    SameSite: http.SameSiteStrictMode,
})
```

In the above, each authenticated request validates the session token with the backend. Invalid or expired tokens prompt re-authentication.

Session Revocation

When you log out, it basically means the system is invalidating your session token and erasing it from both the server and your browser. This makes sure that the risk of session hijacking is minimised, and that access isn't carried forward by accident.

```
func LogoutUser(sessionToken string) {
    removeTokenFromServer(sessionToken)
    // Send cookie deletion response
```

```
}
```

It must clean both server-side and client-side records of the session for airtight security.

There are some pretty cool authentication methods out there these days, like multi-factor authentication (MFA), coding, SMS, and app prompts, which can help keep things more secure. If you track who's trying to log in and audit the authentication logs, you're less likely to be hit by a brute force attack or account takeover.

Password Security

Whenever we welcome a new reader into the Bookstore, we're entrusted with more than just their next favorite book, we're also given their personal credentials. Our job is to guard these secrets with care, so our users always feel safe coming back for more adventures.

Hashing

From the very start, we made a promise never to store plain-text passwords. Instead, each password gets transformed through Go's trusty **bcrypt** package. Bcrypt acts as our invisible shield, scrambling passwords in such a way that nobody (not even us) can piece them back together.

```
import "golang.org/x/crypto/bcrypt"

func hashPassword(password string) (string, error) {

    hash, err := bcrypt.GenerateFromPassword([]byte(password), bcrypt.DefaultCost)

    return string(hash), err

}
```

This line of code becomes part of every registration and password change, a friendly handshake with security.

Salting

Now here, consider that two Bookstore members both pick the password "readmorebooks". If we saved only the hash, an attacker could guess their secret with one lucky strike. But by adding a unique salt, a random jumble of letters and numbers, we guarantee everyone's password protection is one-of-a-kind.

Peppering

On top of salt, we always add a pepper, a secret known only to our server (never stored in the database). This step makes our recipe even tougher for hackers. By changing the pepper every so often, we force even the cleverest attackers to start from scratch.

```
const pepper = "superSecretPepper123"

func hashWithSaltAndPepper(password, salt string) (string, error) {

    scrambled := salt + password + pepper

    hash, err := bcrypt.GenerateFromPassword([]byte(scrambled), bcrypt.DefaultCost)

    return string(hash), err

}
```

With pepper, each password is not just safe, it's resilient against breaches.

When it's time for a reader to log in, we pull their salt and pepper, blend it with their entry, and check if it fits our stored hash, using bcrypt as our taste-tester. A perfect match means access granted, and only then do we let the user back into their Bookstore journey.

In addition, we gently remind users to pick thoughtful passwords, lengthy, creative, and never common. By suggesting, "Why not try a phrase from your favorite book?" we add a dash of Bookstore fun, while keeping their account secure.

Authorization and Access Control

In apps, not every action is made available to every user. The readers can browse, add to their carts, and post reviews, but only admins should update inventory or view detailed sales analytics. This authorization ensures everyone has the right access, keeping features safe and business rules intact.

Roles and Permissions

What if we imagined our users like this? Alice is on the lookout for new fiction, Bob writes reviews, and Carol keeps an eye on the book inventory. The Bookstore just needs to recognise these roles and gently guide each reader to their allowed actions. You only see your own orders, reviewers submit fresh book thoughts and admins get extra dashboards for behind-the-scenes work.

These rules are organised into role-based access control (RBAC), which means every user is assigned a role. It's all linked to the roles, so the code stays readable and if you need to make any changes, it's a piece of cake.

Implementing Access Control

The authentication puts a name to a user, authorization decides "What can they do?" A good access system uses middleware (special code attached to handlers) to check access before any sensitive action proceeds.

Following is a simple example on the middleware for admin-only routes:

```
func AdminOnly(next http.Handler) http.Handler {
    return http.HandlerFunc(func(w http.ResponseWriter, r
*http.Request) {
        user := getUserFromSession(r)
        if user == nil || user.Role != "admin" {
            http.Error(w, "Forbidden", http.StatusForbidden)
            return
        }
        next.ServeHTTP(w, r)
    })
}
// Usage with Gorilla Mux
r.Handle("/inventory/update",
AdminOnly(UpdateInventoryHandler))
```

Here, every time someone clicks to update inventory, the Bookstore quietly double-checks their session and role, only admins go forward.

Fine-Grained Permissions

Sometimes, the roles are not enough; what if only certain reviewers can feature a book? In those cases, permissions are tied to specific actions or resources. For example, we can check whether a user has "feature-book" permission before showing a special button.

```
func HasPermission(user *User, permission string) bool {
    // Check database or in-memory record
    return user.Permissions[permission]
```

```
}
```

The bookstore app offers dashboards (**/admin**), purchase flows (**/buy**), and review pages (**/review**). And, each route receives a custom middleware or permission check. This pattern ensures we never leak sensitive features and can safely add, change, or audit access rules.

By weaving smart authorization checks throughout our app, we keep every Bookstore reader in their lane, safe, empowered, and always one step further in their reading journey.

Integrating OAuth and SSO

As our Bookstore welcomes more readers, the easy sign-in becomes a hallmark of trust and convenience. OAuth and Single Sign-On (SSO) allow users to log in with familiar accounts, Google, Facebook, or others, instead of creating new credentials. This means fewer forgotten passwords and a smoother, more secure entry to every shopping session.

The OAuth is a protocol that lets Bookstore ask a third party to verify a user's identity, without ever seeing their actual password. The process is secure and streamlined: users are redirected to the provider, authenticate there, and return with a token proving their identity. The SSO follows naturally, if a user is logged in to Google, they're instantly recognized on Bookstore as well, skipping extra steps.

Setting up OAuth

First, our Bookstore registers with a provider (e.g., Google) to get its own client ID and client secret. These are used to start OAuth flows, request tokens, and gather user profiles securely.

Following is a simple example on the OAuth config:

```
import (
    "golang.org/x/oauth2"
    "golang.org/x/oauth2/google"
)
var oauthConf = &oauth2.Config{
    ClientID:     "YOUR_CLIENT_ID",
    ClientSecret: "YOUR_CLIENT_SECRET",
    RedirectURL:  "https://bookstore.com/oauth2callback",
    Scopes:       []string{"profile", "email"},
    Endpoint:     google.Endpoint,
```

```
}
```

This config gets used each time a user clicks "Login with Google." Bookstore sends them to the provider's login page.

Handling Redirection and Callbacks

Once the user authenticates with Google, they're returned to Bookstore with an authorization code. Bookstore then exchanges this code for an access token and (often) a refresh token, letting us fetch the user's basic profile.

```
http.HandleFunc("/login", func(w http.ResponseWriter, r
*http.Request) {
    url := oauthConf.AuthCodeURL("state",
oauth2.AccessTypeOffline)
    http.Redirect(w, r, url, http.StatusFound)
})
http.HandleFunc("/oauth2callback", func(w http.ResponseWriter,
r *http.Request) {
    code := r.URL.Query().Get("code")
    token, err := oauthConf.Exchange(r.Context(), code)
    if err != nil {
        http.Error(w, "OAuth Exchange Failed",
http.StatusInternalServerError)
        return
    }
    // Use token to fetch user info, create or update
Bookstore session
})
```

The tokens retrieved from our provider are short-lived and should always be stored with care. And for longer sessions, we can use the refresh tokens to renew access, ensuring the reader stays securely logged in. When Bookstore receives a valid OAuth token, it fetches user profile info (like email or name) and checks if the user already exists in the database. If yes, we log them in and attach a session; if not, we create a new profile. No password ever comes our way, only the provider handles that.

Auditing and Session Security Maintenance

Whenever a reader visits the Bookstore, it's like they're making a trust pact. The thing is, as our system grows, it's easy to miss little quirks in the sessions, expired tokens hanging around, permissions changing, and sensitive data getting mixed up. And auditing makes sure that every session routine stays sharp, verified, and responsive to threats old and new.

Checks during Audits

The audits combine routine health reviews, code inspections, and threat modeling. Together, we watch for:

- Orphaned sessions (those left open after logout or crash).
- Tokens that last too long or drift out of sync.
- Permission creep, when users unintentionally gain extra access after role changes.
- Session store health: expired records, unusual volume, or failed cleanups.

Logging and Monitoring

With every login, logout, permission change, or suspicious attempt, Bookstore notes what happened, when, and by whom. For real-time visibility, we set up alerts for odd patterns, like rapid-fire logins or mismatched tokens, so our team responds quickly instead of piecing together clues days later.

```
func LogSessionEvent(userID int, event string) {

    fmt.Printf("Session event [%s] for user %d at %v\n",
event, userID, time.Now())

}
```

This simple logger attaches to all key session and authentication actions.

Session Expiry, Purge, and Rotation

These tokens shouldn't last forever. All the session cookies have a sensible expiry date, and we track them on both the client- and server-side. During each audit, stale tokens are purged and fresh tokens are issued for sensitive actions (like password changes). We rotate database sessions on a schedule, and swap out session keys regularly to close any lingering vulnerabilities.

```
func PurgeExpiredSessions(db *sql.DB) {

    // Query all sessions; remove any past expiry

}
```

The automation helps here: nightly jobs review and tidy up records, keeping store health and user trust high.

If Bookstore ever spots a breach, auditing logs tell us where, when, and how.

Summary

In this chapter, we've seen how important session management, authentication and authorisation are for making sure web applications are secure and easy to use. We found out how Bookstore used sessions to keep things running smoothly, from persistent carts to personalised recommendations, using both client-side cookies and scalable server-side stores like Redis for flexibility and reliability. We learned to design the login flows to favour bcrypt-hashed passwords, unique salts and peppers, and thoughtful password policies that locked out brute-force attacks. We saw for ourselves how role-based access control and targeted permissions mapped Bookstore features to users, using Go's middleware for seamless guardrails. In the end, all the techniques, from log review to scheduled session key rotations, worked together to create a Bookstore where every user felt safe, recognised and free to explore, protected by security woven into every page and workflow.

CHAPTER 8: FRONTEND AND BACKEND COMMUNICATION

All great web apps are a team effort. In our bookstore, the front end is the cheerful shop window, buttons, forms, curated lists, and vibrant book covers, all inviting users to browse and discover. But behind every click and cart addition is the backend, the silent worker organizing the digital shelves, validating purchases, and updating inventory faster than any librarian ever could. These two sides can really make magic happen when they talk, share data, and create seamless, intuitive experiences.

In this chapter, we're going to take a look at how frontend and backend have been working together more and more, the APIs that connect them, and the patterns every Go developer needs to build apps that respond to the user's needs. No matter how Bookstore's readers buy new releases on their phones or write reviews from their desktops, they can always count on solid communication so their stories won't get interrupted. We're growing, more features, more readers, new integrations, and understanding this communication is key to keeping things fast, secure, and delightful.

The Evolving Role of Frontend and Backend

When you step into the bookstore, you'll see how every click, search, and purchase is made possible by an invisible but crucial team effort. The frontend, or the window of our shop, greets readers with vibrant book covers, smooth navigation, and lively recommendations. But there's a lot going on behind the scenes, like sorting catalogs, handling payments, and keeping accounts safe. The way these two parts work together has changed a lot over the years, making things faster, more flexible, and more personalized than ever before.

Responsibilities Shift

In earlier web projects, the backend handled nearly everything: rendering full pages, making business decisions, even dictating user interfaces. Frontends mostly styled whatever the backend sent, input forms, tables, banners, without much logic of their own. Today, things look very different. Newer JavaScript frameworks and Single Page Applications (SPAs) like React or Vue.js allow the frontend to take on richer tasks. The Bookstore's frontend can filter books, show reviews, and update carts instantly, sometimes with no page reloads at all.

The backend, meanwhile, serves as a reliable engine. It fetches data, validates transactions, manages user sessions, and keeps business rules consistent. The frontend simply asks for what it needs, "Give me the new releases", then takes care of how those books are shown, whether on a phone, tablet, or desktop.

This division makes upgrading features a breeze. The designers reshape menus or animations directly in the frontend, while backend teams optimize queries or introduce new logic underneath. Each team innovates separately, confident the API binds their work together.

Real-Time Communication and APIs

What really supercharges this relationship? APIs. Instead of direct lines between database and browser, APIs act as gatekeepers, offering clean, documented endpoints. For the Bookstore, when a reader searches for "Go programming," the frontend sends a request to a backend API, gets structured results, and displays recommendations. The backend answers with only the necessary data, no clutter, no confusion, often using JSON for clarity and consistency. This API-driven connection means Bookstore can launch mobile apps, browser extensions, and integrations with partner sites, all fueling the same backend.

With responsibilities clarified and APIs as connectors, the Bookstore can grow, without tangled code or unpredictable surprises. We should keep in mind that it's not just about technology, but about making readers happy. A well-balanced frontend and backend lets us serve every customer better, growing our Bookstore from a single shelf to a global library, one seamless experience at a time.

Designing & Building Reliable APIs

It's time to take charge. We know that bookstore readers want quick search results, easy checkouts, and smart reviews, whether they're on a phone, desktop, or using a digital assistant. As API designers, our job is to make sure the frontend always gets what it needs in a clear, predictable format. This way, designers and developers can move fast and add features without fear.

Structuring API

The RESTful APIs revolve around resources. In Bookstore, these resources might be books, reviews, orders, or users. Each has its own endpoint:

- **`GET /books`** – List all books
- **`GET /books/{id}`** – See details of a single book
- **`POST /orders`** – Place an order
- **`PUT /users/{id}`** – Update a profile

This clear pattern helps frontend colleagues know exactly where to ask for data, and keeps our code organized.

We will try a Go structure together:

```
import (
    "net/http"
    "github.com/gorilla/mux"
)
func main() {
```

```
    r := mux.NewRouter()
    r.HandleFunc("/books", GetBooks).Methods("GET")
    r.HandleFunc("/books/{id}", GetBook).Methods("GET")
    r.HandleFunc("/orders", CreateOrder).Methods("POST")
    http.ListenAndServe(":8080", r)
}
```

Here, we are using the Gorilla Mux for friendly routing. Each handler focuses on a single job, keeping code easy to test and maintain.

Clear Responses, Good Errors

In the handlers, we decode requests, check permissions, fetch or update data, and return JSON that's formatted just right. It's pretty straightforward: real-world bookstore handlers include helpful status codes, and when something goes wrong (like a missing book ID), they always send a clear error the frontend can use.

```
func GetBook(w http.ResponseWriter, r *http.Request) {
    vars := mux.Vars(r)
    id := vars["id"]
    book, err := fetchBookByID(id)
    if err != nil {
        http.Error(w, `{"error":"Book not found"}`,
http.StatusNotFound)
        return
    }
    json.NewEncoder(w).Encode(book)
}
```

All responses, the good and the bad, stick to a contract so the frontend never has to guess.

Security, Logging, and Reusability

We have explored that the middlewares are like trusted assistants. We use them for:

- Logging each request.
- Checking authentication tokens.

- Handling CORS for frontend development.
- Managing rate limits or IP bans.

All this keeps business logic clean and enforces good practices everywhere.

```
func LoggingMiddleware(next http.Handler) http.Handler {
    return http.HandlerFunc(func(w http.ResponseWriter, r
*http.Request) {
        log.Printf("Request: %s %s", r.Method, r.URL.Path)
        next.ServeHTTP(w, r)
    })
}
```

We can then attach the middleware as below:

```
r.Use(LoggingMiddleware)
```

To try littleharder, you may try adding a route to let users save "favorite" books. We have to sketch the endpoint (resource & method), update the handler, and also then to extend the API contract.

JSON as the Language of Web Data

Whenever the Bookstore's frontend asks the backend for new books, hot reviews, or cart contents, there's a translation happening behind the scenes. It's basically a universal language that everyone can understand. It's compact, easy to read, and works well with browsers, Go servers, and even third-party APIs.

And whether they're on a phone or a desktop, the Bookstore's backend returns data in JSON. We're able to give you a format that's as easy for machines as it is for people, and sometimes even readers looking over their browser's network tab can see it.

Structuring and Tagging

Let's create a Book structure for our API. The struct tags are what align backend fields with the expected frontend names:

```
type Book struct {
    ID     int     `json:"id"`
    Title  string  `json:"title"`
```

```
    Author string  `json:"author"`
    Price  float64 `json:"price"`
}
```

Now here, you must notice how each field gets a **`json:"..."`** tag? This ensures the API sends and receives data that always matches the frontend's expectations, no confusion, no broken UI.

Encoding Data for API Responses

Say that we've pulled a list of books from the database and want to give it to the web frontend. Following is how we do it:

```
func sendBooks(w http.ResponseWriter, books []Book) {
    w.Header().Set("Content-Type", "application/json")
    if err := json.NewEncoder(w).Encode(books); err != nil {
        http.Error(w, "error encoding JSON",
http.StatusInternalServerError)
    }
}
```

Here, there is no need to handcraft JSON strings or stress over escaping. We can tell Go what to send, and it will simply do the entire heavy lifting.

Decoding JSON Requests

Similarly, when a user adds a review or updates a shopping cart, the frontend posts JSON to the backend. Our handlers decode it into Go structs as shown below:

```
func addBook(w http.ResponseWriter, r *http.Request) {
    var newBook Book
    if err := json.NewDecoder(r.Body).Decode(&newBook); err !=
nil {
        http.Error(w, "bad request", http.StatusBadRequest)
        return
    }
    // Now use newBook (already validated and mapped)
```

```
}
```

The decoding handles everything, including the unexpected fields are ignored, and the missing required ones are caught for smart error handling.

With its thoughtful JSON structure and clear contracts, the Bookstore connects frontend and backend with clarity and speed, making sure every reader has a consistent experience on any platform or feature.

Efficient Data Fetching and Pagination

Now there will be situations wherein there will be suddenly like twenty books become twenty thousand. So here, if our API tries returning every title in a single response, the browser will crawl, data plans will cry, and the user will flee. This is where the pagination lets us serve books, reviews, or orders in tidy slices. It helps keeping apps fast, predictable, and fun to browse.

The navigation behavior of readers is that they don't want to scroll through endless lists. Instead, they expect:

- The first page right away ("Show me the newest releases!"),
- A "Next" button (or infinite scroll) for more,
- The ability to filter by author, genre, or price,
- Quick load times, even with complex queries.

Behind the scenes, our API must handle all these requests gracefully, fetching just enough data, and telling the frontend what's available next.

Offset and Limit

This is a go-to for simple lists. The frontend sends two parameters, one is **`page`** (or **`offset`**) and the other is **`limit`** (how many items per page).

Following is a sample API call:

```
GET /books?page=2&limit=10
```

The backend grabs books 11 through 20 from the database and responds with:

```
{
  "books": [...],
  "total": 203,
  "page": 2,
  "limit": 10
```

```
}
```

With this, the frontend knows exactly how many more pages can be shown. The following is a sample program on Go Handler:

```
func GetBooks(w http.ResponseWriter, r *http.Request) {
    page, _ := strconv.Atoi(r.URL.Query().Get("page"))
    limit, _ := strconv.Atoi(r.URL.Query().Get("limit"))
    if page < 1 { page = 1 }
    if limit < 1 || limit > 50 { limit = 10 }
    offset := (page - 1) * limit
    books, total := fetchBookPage(offset, limit)
    json.NewEncoder(w).Encode(map[string]interface{}{
        "books": books,
        "total": total,
        "page": page,
        "limit": limit,
    })
}
```

Filtering and Searching

The Bookstore's API doesn't stop at pagination. It lets readers zero in.

- Filter by genre: /books?genre=Sci-Fi&page=1&limit=10
- Search by keyword: /books?q=concurrency
- Combine filters: /reviews?userId=22&stars=5

On the backend, parsed query parameters steer SQL or ORM queries, returning exactly what's needed, no more, no less.

Every Bookstore paginated endpoint returns:

- The current page (or cursor info),
- Number of results per page,
- Total results (if possible),
- Links or tokens for fetching more.

This empowers the frontend to build infinite scrolling, page indicators, and "load more" buttons that never frustrate users.

Asynchronous and Concurrent API Patterns

What if a reader logs in and wants to see their book recommendations, cart items, and active discussions all at once? If we process each request in sequence, it'll slow things down, especially as Bookstore scales. Then there are Go's goroutines and channels. With just a bit of code, we can launch parallel data fetches, handle slow services with grace, and serve lightning-fast responses that delight even your busiest users.

Starting Multiple Fetches

How about we build a scenario? The bookstore's API should deliver a dashboard with recommendations, latest reviews, and a "last seen" list. So instead of pinging each service one at a time (and making our frontend wait), we spin up a goroutine for every fetch and sync results back with channels:

```
type DashboardData struct {
    Recommendations []Book
    RecentReviews   []Review
    LastSeen        []Book
    // ... add more as needed!
}
func fetchDashboard(userID int) DashboardData {
    recCh := make(chan []Book)
    revCh := make(chan []Review)
    lastSeenCh := make(chan []Book)
    go func() { recCh <- getRecommendations(userID) }()
    go func() { revCh <- getRecentReviews(userID) }()
    go func() { lastSeenCh <- getLastSeenBooks(userID) }()
    // Wait for all results
    return DashboardData{
        Recommendations: <-recCh,
        RecentReviews:   <-revCh,
```

```
        LastSeen:       <-lastSeenCh,
    }
}
```

With this, the Bookstore delivers three fresh data sets in the time it would usually take to fetch just one. The user gets their dashboard, and that too instantly responsive.

Handling Errors Gracefully

In the real world, not every service answers on time. We can use a struct or error type to pass both successful and failed fetches through the channel:

```
type Result[T any] struct {
    Data T
    Err  error
}
```

After this, we can read from each channel, and if something fails, we can return the partial data with a user-friendly error.

WaitGroups for Aggregation

For more dynamic API calls, where we are not sure how many sources to query, sync everything cleanly with a **sync.WaitGroup**:

```
var wg sync.WaitGroup
for _, src := range sources {
    wg.Add(1)
    go func(src Source) {
        defer wg.Done()
        processSource(src)
    }(src)
}
wg.Wait()
```

This guarantees every concurrent job finishes before we respond.

Timeout and Cancellation

Generally, we must not let a single slow backend grind Bookstore to a halt! We need to wrap the goroutines in **context.WithTimeout** and watch for channel timeouts:

```
ctx, cancel := context.WithTimeout(context.Background(),
2*time.Second)
defer cancel()
select {
case data := <-fetchCh:
    // handle success
case <-ctx.Done():
    // handle timeout, maybe use cached or default data
}
```

If you can master these async and concurrent patterns, our Bookstore backend can scale with certainty, delivering personalization and freshness in a fraction of the time, and never letting sluggish services disappoint your readers.

API Authentication and Authorization

Whenever the Bookstore frontend connects with the backend, like when adding a review or fetching orders, there's a chance of exposure. A lot of sensitive user data is handled by APIs, and without tight authentication and authorization, even well-designed endpoints can become soft targets. There's always the chance that a scammer could pretend to be a user, steal private details, or mess with transactions. That's why it's crucial to have solid API identity checks and permission enforcement right from the start.

Token-based Authentication

The tokens, especially the JSON Web Tokens (JWT), are the backbone of secure API authentication. When a user logs in or registers, Bookstore generates a signed JWT embedding their user ID (and, optionally, their roles or permissions). That token acts as a digital passport, sent along with every API call in an **Authorization** header.

Following is a token generation sample program:

```
import "github.com/dgrijalva/jwt-go"
func GenerateToken(userID string) (string, error) {
```

```
    token := jwt.NewWithClaims(jwt.SigningMethodHS256,
jwt.MapClaims{
        "userID": userID,
    })
    return token.SignedString([]byte("your-secret-key"))
}
```

Now here, during each request, the backend checks the signature, verifies it's untampered, then reads embedded user data straight from the token. There is no repeated password checks required.

Protecting Endpoints with Middleware

If you're dealing with sensitive stuff like posting a review, managing orders, or updating a user profile, you need to use middleware that checks for a valid token and authorized role or action. It keeps business logic neat and security centralized.

Let's look at an example of Authentication Middleware below:

```
func AuthMiddleware(next http.Handler) http.Handler {
    return http.HandlerFunc(func(w http.ResponseWriter, r
*http.Request) {
        tokenString := r.Header.Get("Authorization")
        // Token validation logic (decode, verify, extract
claims) here.
        userID, err := ValidateToken(tokenString)
        if err != nil {
            http.Error(w, "Invalid or expired token",
http.StatusUnauthorized)
            return
        }
        // Store user info in context if needed.
        next.ServeHTTP(w, r)
    })
}
```

After this, just wrap any route you want to lock down:

```
r.Handle("/orders",
AuthMiddleware(CreateOrderHandler)).Methods("POST")
```

With this, our Bookstore is abel to keep every transaction and interaction private, correct, and trustworthy. It thereby makes the security as smooth and natural as browsing the latest bestsellers.

Integrating External APIs and Services

Sometimes, the best feature isn't one you build from scratch, it's one we borrow, connect, or extend. The Bookstore could wow our readers by offering detailed book metadata, payment gateways, or curated reviews from platforms like Goodreads or Open Library. That's where the external APIs come in. They let us focus on what makes Bookstore unique, while leaning on experts for specialized data and services.

Choosing External API

Before plugging in a new service, we must ask ourselves:

- Is it reliable, up-to-date, and well-documented?
- Are there rate limits, quotas, or costs?
- Does it support the formats (like JSON) and authentication Bookstore already uses?
- How is support for security, API key management, and error handling?

The best APIs make integration smooth, upgrades regular, and debugging easier down the road.

External Communication

The Go's **`net/http`** package makes connecting to third-party APIs clean and fun:

```
func GetBookSummary(bookID string) (string, error) {
    url :=
fmt.Sprintf("https://booksummaryapi.com/summary/%s", bookID)
    resp, err := http.Get(url)
    if err != nil {
        return "", err
    }
    defer resp.Body.Close()
```

```go
    if resp.StatusCode != http.StatusOK {
        return "", fmt.Errorf("bad response: %s", resp.Status)
    }
    body, _ := ioutil.ReadAll(resp.Body)
    return string(body), nil
}
```

This example fetches a summary, which is ready to enrich any book detail page, right in the user's browser or app.

Handling Rate Limits and Reliability

We also know that certain external services often set request caps per second or day. We need to respect these rules to avoid disruptions, using Go's **`time.Ticker`** or more advanced throttling libraries to space calls. On hitting a rate limit or temporary outage, Bookstore can queue requests, use cached data, or show friendly "please try again later" messages.

```go
ticker := time.NewTicker(time.Second)
// Use ticker.C to space API calls
```

All these integrates external APIs in a smart way, delivering more value and features with less work. It's always secure, reliable, and ready to adapt to the ever-changing world outside its own digital shelves.

Summary

To sum it up, we saw how the Bookstore's frontend and backend split into different layers that work well together, with each layer having its own area but connected by API-driven architecture. We learned to design RESTful APIs with clean routing and modular handlers, and everyone used JSON for reliable data contracts. It's got practical coding and everyday examples that make it clear why pagination, filtering, and structured responses matter, whether you're fetching thousands of book records or narrowing by genre. We learned about concurrency and goroutines, which helped us scale out dramatic dashboard fetches, delivering speedy answers and graceful error handling even with slow or flaky services.

We figured out how to use API authentication and authorization, build secure endpoints using JWTs and middleware, and protect every sensitive flow with careful role checks. It's really important to test continuously, keep an eye on things, have good contracts, and roll out new versions safely. This lets the platform grow without any problems, and we're happy with how things are going.

CHAPTER 9: TESTING AND DEBUGGING

These days, even small Go web apps can quickly grow to serve thousands of readers and spin up dozens of dependencies. With that kind of scale, there are always surprises around the corner: a typo messes up the checkout process, a forgotten edge case crashes a handler, or a change upstream wreaks havoc on your API. So, what's the answer? We all treat quality like a team sport.

It's not something we do on the side or in our free time. These are things we do every day to keep Bookstore strong. The best engineers and the healthiest teams are always looking at what's going "under the hood." They write and run tests, check logs, tighten performance, and make sure every new feature is protected against regressions. This way, people have more energy for creative work, feel less stressed at night, and make sure that the code they leave is a little stronger than when they started.

Quality-Driven Mindset

If you think of Bookstore as a real shop, you'll see what I mean. If the shelves are messy or the receipts are glitchy, customers leave. When it comes to quality in code, the goal is simple: the checkout process works, everyone gets the right book, and the site is ready for the holiday rush. In practice, this mindset is all about catching mistakes early, making improvements with confidence, and never guessing if a change broke something that worked yesterday.

Let's say you're adding a new book filter feature. Maybe you write this function:

```
func FilterBooksByGenre(books []Book, genre string) []Book {
/* ... */ }
```

A quality-driven dev doesn't just write the function and push it to production. You write a test first:

```
func TestFilterBooksByGenre(t *testing.T) {

    books := []Book{{Title: "Go Basics", Genre: "Tech"},
{Title: "Cooking", Genre: "Food"}}

    result := FilterBooksByGenre(books, "Tech")

    if len(result) != 1 || result[0].Title != "Go Basics" {

        t.Fatalf("expected 1 tech book")

    }

}
```

Now, if you ever refactor that function or change how genres are stored, this test has your back. A failing test means you can fix the bug before it hits real readers.

Say you want to speed up the search endpoint. A quality-minded team profiles the handler, spots a slow SQL query, rewrites it, and always adds a test or check to ensure it's still correct and now faster.

Unit, Integration, and End-to-End Testing

Let's say we update the Bookstore's checkout logic. How do we explore every blind spot, could a math error sneak onto a cart total? Do the discount rules apply to every book? I'm wondering if the change will break the page in Safari, or if it'll only happen when the user's cart is empty. Each of these needs a different test to be caught early, not in production.

Unit Tests

Each unit test focuses on just one function. It doesn't have any databases or web servers, just logic in and logic out. They're super fast and cover every base.

Suppose we have:

```
func CalculateTotal(books []Book, discount float64) float64 {
/* ... */ }
```

So here, a table-driven test zooms in:

```
func TestCalculateTotal(t *testing.T) {
    cases := []struct {
        books    []Book
        discount float64
        want     float64
    }{
        {[]Book{{Price: 10}}, 0.1, 9},
        {[]Book{}, 0.2, 0},
    }
    for _, c := range cases {
        got := CalculateTotal(c.books, c.discount)
        if got != c.want {
            t.Errorf("got %f, want %f", got, c.want)
        }
```

```
    }
}
```

Now, if a future change slips up the math, this test heads it off in seconds.

Integration Tests

After this, the integration tests make sure pieces fit together. They connect to a real or mock database, check handler–middleware interactions, and see how Bookstore acts when a cart is submitted for a user who is (or isn't) logged in.

For example:

```
func TestCheckoutWorkflow(t *testing.T) {
    mockDB := NewMockDB()
    server := httptest.NewServer(AppWithDB(mockDB))
    defer server.Close()
    resp, err := http.Post(server.URL+"/checkout",
"application/json", bytes.NewReader(orderJSON))
    // Now check response, mockDB.calls, etc.
}
```

They catch bugs that individual units miss, like an endpoint returning 404 because of a tiny routing typo.

End-to-End Tests

The E2E tests act like a real user, so they'll open the browser, click "add to cart," fill in an address, checkout, and check for an order confirmation. There are tools like Selenium, Cypress, and Playwright that can help you script the whole flow.

The thing is, this only finds failures when the frontend, backend, database, and browser all line up. Yes, E2E tests are slower, but catching "it broke in the real world" moments saves you pain on release day.

For example, a Cypress test logs in, browses a book, and checks that a purchase button works (and doesn't for guests).

And if our Bookstore feature only has unit tests, try adding an integration test that sets up a mock database or service. And for high-traffic or important flows, try out an E2E tool, even scripting a "buy" from the homepage to confirmation. It's important to be aware of which bugs each level catches, and combining all three means you won't have any surprises for your users.

Mocking, Fakes, and Isolated Environments

Referring to the previous topic, if every unit test depended on a real database or hit a third-party API, your feedback loop would grind to a halt. The tests might fail when the database goes down or the API is slow. Mocking solves this by letting you "pretend" those dependencies behave in a controlled way, so you can focus on your code logic instead of outside services.

Mocking with Go Interfaces

In Go, the mocking is easy because of interfaces. Let us consider that the service fetches the book details:

```
type Database interface {
    FetchBookByID(id int) (Book, error)
}
```

You can make a lightweight mock, like so:

```
type MockDatabase struct {
    Books map[int]Book
}
func (m *MockDatabase) FetchBookByID(id int) (Book, error) {
    book, ok := m.Books[id]
    if !ok {
        return Book{}, fmt.Errorf("not found")
    }
    return book, nil
}
```

In our test, we then pass the mock into our handler:

```
func TestGetBook(t *testing.T) {
    db := &MockDatabase{Books: map[int]Book{1: {Title: "Go in
Action"}}}
    book, err := db.FetchBookByID(1)
    require.NoError(t, err)
```

```
    require.Equal(t, "Go in Action", book.Title)
}
```

After this, our test doesn't depend on any environment except our test double.

Mocking External Services

If Bookstore works with a review API, for example:

```
type ReviewAPI interface {
    FetchReviewsForBook(id int) (Review, error)
}
type MockReviewAPI struct{ Reviews map[int]Review }
func (m *MockReviewAPI) FetchReviewsForBook(id int) (Review,
error) {
    return m.Reviews[id], nil
}
```

By doing as above, you're in full control of the test world. And we will never risk hitting real network limits or getting charged for test calls.

Debugging, Tracing, and Structured Logging

Every Go application, including Bookstore, has hidden adventures happening every second: a user searches for a rare book, an order fails, a review gets posted. If something goes wrong, say, a payment service is down, or a user can't find their order, logs and traces help developers "rewind the tape" and see exactly what happened, when, and for whom.

Smart Logging

The logging isn't about having walls of unreadable output or endless "Something broke!" messages. The good logs tell a story: what the system was doing, for whom, and what went wrong (or right). And for this, the **`log`** package is the starting point:

```
log.Printf("orderID=%d, userID=%d, status=%s", orderID,
userID, status)
```

This kind of log gives real context, a developer can trace a problem back to its root without digging aimlessly.

For richer systems, use structured loggers like Logrus and Zap. These provide machine-parsable logs (often JSON), making it easier to slice, dice, and aggregate data:

```
log.WithFields(log.Fields{
    "orderID": orderID,
    "userID":  userID,
    "status":  status,
}).Error("order processing error")
```

These logs are perfect for pulling into dashboards, setting up alerts, and auditing suspicious activity.

Request and Trace Context

What if a user says it was slow for them, but you can't reproduce the issue? When you get an incoming request, attach a unique request ID to it. Your log and trace system syncs this ID across HTTP handlers, database queries, and even outgoing API calls. Now, you can see the whole journey of that request, helping diagnose latency issues, timeouts, or misrouted data.

```
ctx := context.WithValue(r.Context(), "requestID", uuid.New())
```

Your middleware can inject this ID automatically, ensuring every piece of the stack "speaks the same language" when recording activity or errors.

Performance Testing and Profiling

No one likes a laggy Bookstore, whether it's a reader waiting for search results or an admin updating prices. Even code that "works" can waste resources or slow down as data grows. The concept of profiling and performance benchmarking brings a spotlight on the slowest corners of our code, so we fix real bottlenecks and ship features with confidence.

Go's Profiling Toolkit

I won't hesitate to say again but Go comes with everything you need out of the box:

- **CPU Profile**: Find out where your app spends the most "compute" time.
- **Memory Profile**: Discover why your RAM spikes or where memory leaks may happen.
- **Block/Profile**: See where goroutines, network calls, or database queries get stuck waiting.

Following is how to try a quick CPU profile:

```
import (
    "runtime/pprof"
    "os"
)
// At the start of main:
f, _ := os.Create("cpu.pprof")
pprof.StartCPUProfile(f)
defer pprof.StopCPUProfile()
```

We then run the app, then analyze with:

```
go tool pprof cpu.pprof
```

After this, you'll see a "top" of your slowest functions, these are your golden tuning targets.

Memory Profiling and Leaks

These memory leaks mess with the performance and load times. To catch them:

```
f, _ := os.Create("mem.pprof")
pprof.WriteHeapProfile(f)
f.Close()
```

Here, you need to look for unclosed channels, long-lived goroutines, or big cached objects that should be evicted.

Benchmarking Functions

And how about if a code change really speeds things up? For such things, the **`go test`** makes it easy:

```
func BenchmarkCalculateTotal(b *testing.B) {
    books := makeSampleBooks()
    for i := 0; i < b.N; i++ {
        CalculateTotal(books, 0.1)
    }
```

```
}
```

Let Go run your function thousands of times and report "best/worst/average" timing. Now, you can track improvements and make sure "simpler code" doesn't secretly slow something down.

Production-Ready Error Response Playbook

For example, if something goes wrong in the bookstore, like a payment doesn't go through, there's low inventory, or an API times out, we'll let users know in a helpful way, but we'll never share any sensitive details. The best error responses don't show raw stack traces or SQL errors. Instead, they show gentle, helpful messages while the system logs the gritty details for the team.

Here's a friendly API error response:

```
{
    "error": "The requested book is out of stock. Please check again soon or contact support."
}
```

And the Bookstore actually logs the following:

```
orderID=202483, userID=554, error="stock=0 after attempted purchase"
```

With this, users aren't frustrated or scared, and the ops team can track, investigate, and resolve issues fast.

With regardsd to the error, whether in JSON API or an HTML response, every error should have:

- A clear short message ("Invalid login credentials", "Cart expired")
- An internal error code or request ID for supporting staff
- (Optional) Suggestion/fallback ("Try placing your order again," or "Reset your password")
- NEVER include secrets, raw details, or system internals in user-facing messages

When certain errors happen, like too many failed logins, database timeouts, or payment rejections, the system should automatically log and alert. We can use the error aggregation tools (Sentry, Rollbar, PagerDuty, or just Slack bots) to notify the right team without overwhelming them with noise.

Following is the sample alert:

"ALERT: 10+ failed logins for user 8810 in last 3 minutes. Possible brute force attack."

It's not about avoiding all outages, but about how quickly and transparently you respond to them. And here's how Bookstore's strategy shakes out:

1. The first responder checks the dashboard or alert. Is it backend, payments, accounts? Categorize the issue, big, small, user-impacting?
2. Update the Bookstore status page and, if wide-impact, notify support staff with a templated status message.
3. Use logs (with request IDs), traces, and live metrics to pinpoint when and where the failure started.
4. If needed, disable the troubled feature, throttle requests, or apply a circuit breaker until a fix is in place.
5. Once resolved, document what happened, how it was fixed, and what new checks or alerts will catch the issue sooner next time.
6. Let users and partners know it's safe to return, and offer an apology or follow-up as needed.

It's all about making sure the bookstore's error responses are on point, human, safe, and logged properly. And, of course, the team's got a solid playbook for any hiccups. That way, no bug or outage goes from bad to worse. This helps users stay calm, fixes issues faster, and ensures the shelf won't stay empty for long.

Summary

In short, we saw how a quality-driven mindset influenced every step of Bookstore's growth. They used real tests, meaningful logs, and clear error handling to build a project that could easily scale and handle surprises. We saw the value of fast unit tests, thorough integration exercises, and end-to-end flows, making sure new features and existing logic stayed reliable while code changed. Techniques like mocking and fakes let them separate their tests from real databases and APIs, speeding up feedback and catching bugs before launch. We learned how to use profiling tools to find the slow functions and memory leaks, which let the developers optimize Bookstore for busy sales days. Ultimately, these classes provided Bookstore with a solid base of trust, growth, and consistent excellence.

Index

P

R

S

T

U

V

X

Epilogue

So, as you reach this section, I am assuming you have completed the book read, and believe that you've got the working code, and a better idea of what it means to create web applications that people trust and enjoy. We've explored examples and practices for every kind of project, from the simple to the ambitious, and every one is built from habits, decisions and moments of curiosity. All the challenges you've taken on here are real-life work stuff, and the fact that you've stuck with it, adapted and pushed on is proof that the most important thing is just to get started.

If you keep coming back to certain topics, improving features, or teaching others these patterns, remember that every time you build, you'll come up with a few more creative solutions. There'll always be new libraries to explore, bugs to squash, and user needs to understand—but you'll be ready to meet them head-on, with the confidence you'll gain through hands-on practice.

I really appreciate you taking part in this process, asking questions and putting in the time to develop your own skills and perspective. Next time you make a web app, whether for yourself, your team or the world, it'll be even better because of what you know now. The best thing is seeing your work run, grow, and maybe even inspire someone else to start using Go.

Thank You

www.ingramcontent.com/pod-product-compliance
Lightning Source LLC
Chambersburg PA
CBHW080215170726
48282CB00030B/1127
* 9 7 8 9 3 4 9 1 7 4 3 0 6 *